KB131310

저절로 외워지는 하루 10분 영어 공부

빈틈없는 입체 반복 영어 60일의 기적

저절로 외워지는 하루 10분 영어 공부

초판 1쇄 발행 2018년 11월 5일 초판 3쇄 발행 2020년 3월 9일

지은이 유세라 펴낸이 연준혁

편집 1본부 본부장 배민수
뉴북 팀장 조한나
디자인 HADA 장선숙

펴낸곳 (주)위즈덤하우스 미디어그룹 출판등록 2000년 5월 23일 제13-1071호
주소 경기도 고양시 일산동구 장항동 846번지 센트럴프라자 6층
전화 031)936-4000 팩스 031)903-3893 홈페이지 www.wisdomhouse.co.kr

값 14,000원 ISBN 979-11-6220-953-0 13740

빈틈없는 입체 반복 영어 60일의 기적

저절로 외워지는 하루 10분 영어 공부

유세라 지음

위즈덤하우스

왜 영어 표현을 외워도 실전에서 써먹지 못할까요?

도대체 왜 머리 밖으로 안 꺼내지죠?

★ 한국인에게 꽂히는 표현 ★

표현을 고르고 예문을 쓸 때 저는 연기자가 됩니다.
"내 말투인가?" "자연스러운가?"
"실제 상황에서 딱 떠오를 만큼 쉬운가?"

많은 분들이 "표현을 외워도 말할 때 떠오르지 않는다"고 고민합니다. 살펴보면, 수준에 맞지 않는 고급 표현들을 사용하려고 하거나, 실제 사용빈도가 낮은 표현들을 붙잡고 씨름하는 경우가 많습니다.

이 책의 시작은 기초회화 학습자를 위한 **'스피킹 영단어 특강'**이었습니다. 수업 자료를 만들 때마다 머릿속으로 되뇌며 다짐한 것이 있습니다.
영어 지식 자랑하지 말자. 입말에 집중하자.
보기 좋은 떡이 맛도 좋다지만, 영어 말하기만큼은 보기에는 좋지만 뜯어먹기 힘든 표현이 많다는 것을 경험을 통해 알고 있습니다. 길어야 하루 한 시간 투자하게 될 바쁜 학습자들이 쉽게 익혀 바로 쓸 수 있는 심플하고 유용한 표현을 뽑았습니다.

머릿속이 전쟁을 방불케 할 실전 영어 상황에서
❶ **이 책에서 배운 표현이 기억나**서,
❷ 그것을 **주어(I) 뒤에 척 갖다 붙여 여러 번 연습**했더니,
❸ **영어 대화가 되더라**는 리얼 체험 후기를 들을 수 있는 표현을 엄선하자.
어떻게? 바로 이 책을 쓰기로 마음 먹은 이유입니다.

★ '동사구 표현'을 싣자 ★

영어로 말해봅시다.
'어머, 나 실수했어'

my mistake, my mistake(내 실수, 내 실수) × ··· **단어**로만 소통하는 나쁜 습관
I mistook(나 실수했어) × ··· 한국말 그대로 번역해서 쓰는 틀린 표현
I made a mistake(나 실수했어) ○ ··· **'실수하다'**는 make a mistake

make a mistake를 '**실수하다**' 동사구 덩어리로 알아두면 쉽게 만들 수 있는 영어식 문장이죠. 이렇게 표현들을 동사구로 알아두면, 주어 뒤에 적절하게 붙이기만 하면 되니 문장이 뒤죽박죽 될 걱정, 콩글리시를 말할 걱정이 없지요. 한번 비교해볼까요?

비교해보기

개별단어 암기	동사구 암기
스트레칭(stretching)	스트레칭 하다(do stretching)
다이어트(diet)	다이어트하다(go on a diet)
쇼핑(shopping)	쇼핑하다(go shopping)
주연(lead role)	주연을 맡다(play the lead role)
인맥(network)	인맥을 넓히다(expand my network)
아르바이트(part-time)	아르바이트하다(work part-time)

어떤가요? 우리말로는 같은 '하다'지만, 영어에서는 스트레칭을 '하다', 다이어트를 '하다' 등 명사에 따라 다양한 동사를 사용하지요? 이젠 단어만 외우지 말고 '동사구'를 알아두도록 합시다. 이 책은 배운 표현을 실전에서 바로 문장으로 만들어 사용할 수 있도록 실생활 단골 동사구 표현들을 주로 수록했습니다.

★ '친숙한 표현'을 싣자 ★

영어로 말해볼까요?

나는 **가정적인 남자**가 좋아요. ··· I like a **family-oriented guy**.
목표 지향적인 사람들이 매력 있더라. ··· I think **goal-oriented people** are attractive.

가정적인 남자, 목표 지향적인 사람들…
처음엔 어려워 보이지만, 들여다보면 한국인이 콩글리시처럼 자주 쓰는 단어들의 조합이에요. 가족(family), 목표(goal)에 (-oriented)만 붙여주면 되는 간단한 패턴이지요. 쉬운 단어들의 조합이라 알아두면 말할 때 잘 떠오르는 건 덤이고요. 이와 같이 기존의 익숙한 각 단어들을 잘 이어 쉽게 기억할 수 있는 실용 표현들을 포착해 수록했습니다.

★ 일상생활 표현을 주제별로 담아라 ★

직장생활, **건강관리**, **자기계발**, **육아**, **쇼핑**…….
일상생활에서 대화거리로 자주 등장하는 주제들을 모두 담아, 관심 있는 주제부터 선택해서 정복해 나갈 수 있도록 구성했습니다. 순서대로 공부할 수도 있겠지만, 내 일상과 연관된 주제부터 공부하고, 실생활에 바로 적용해봐도 좋겠습니다. 연구에 따르면, 주어진 문장을 기계적으로 암기하는 것은 효율적이지 않다고 합니다. 본인에게 유용한 표현을 선택하고 문장에 넣어 내 말투로 직접 말해보거나, 상대방과 대화 연습을 통해 표현을 '자기화'하는 것이 가장 효율적인 말하기 훈련입니다.

★ 오감 활용, 빈틈없는 반복학습 ★
〈 이해 → 영작 → 테스트 → 쓰기 → 대화 〉

영어 표현을 이해만 하고, 듣고 써보지 않으면 어떻게 될까요? 배운 내용이 단기 기억장소에만 잠시 머물다 흩어질 겁니다. 말하기를 공부하는 학습자에게는 문장으로 써보고, 들어보고, 상황에 맞게 떠올려보는 능동적인 학습이 반드시 필요합니다. 직접 써보고 고쳐봐야 사소한 실수들을 잡아낼 수 있습니다.
펜을 들고 직접 끄적여보고, 듣고 받아 써볼 수 있도록 책에 여백을 두는 구성을 했습니다. 책에 제시된 방법으로 공부했을 때, 여러분은 한 표현당 적어도 3번은 눈과 귀와 손으로 반복하게 될 겁니다. 또한 여러 미디어 학습자료를 제공해 여러 번 더 반복하도록 하였습니다. 영어는 반복입니다. 좋은 표현을 듣고 쓰고 말하는 반복 훈련을 할 수 있도록 잘 차려놓았습니다. 이제 여러분이 할 일은 60일 간 이 책을 믿고 따라오는 것입니다.

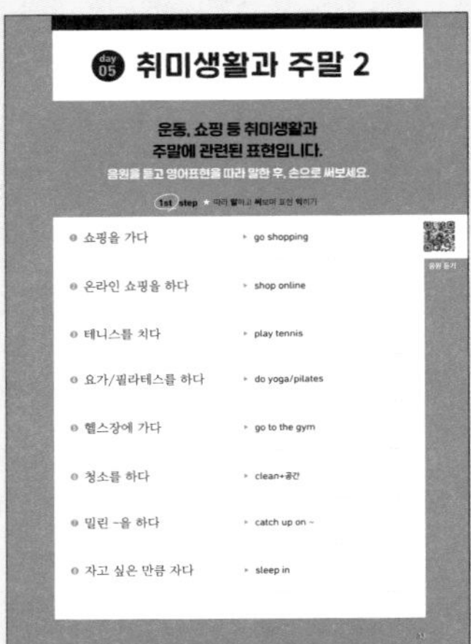
day 05 취미생활과 주말 2

운동, 쇼핑 등 취미생활과
주말에 관련된 표현입니다.
음원을 듣고 영어표현을 따라 말한 후, 손으로 써보세요.

1st step

쇼핑을 가다	go shopping
온라인 쇼핑을 하다	shop online
테니스를 치다	play tennis
요가/필라테스를 하다	do yoga/pilates
헬스장에 가다	go to the gym
청소를 하다	clean+공간
밀린 ~을 하다	catch up on ~
자고 싶은 만큼 자다	sleep in

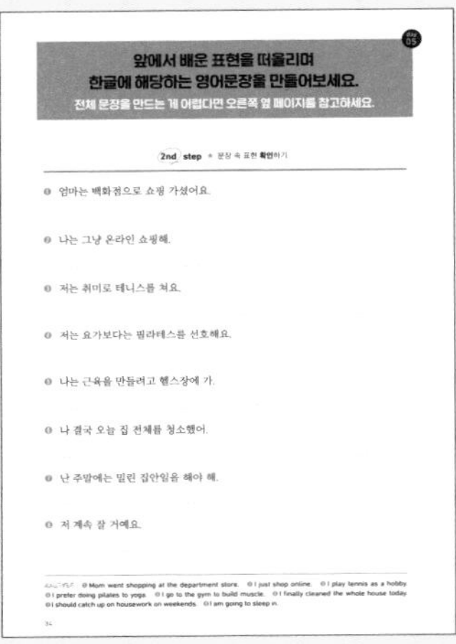
앞에서 배운 표현을 떠올리며
한글에 해당하는 영어문장을 만들어보세요.
전체 문장을 만드는 게 어렵다면 오른쪽 옆 페이지를 참고하세요.

2nd step

- 엄마는 백화점으로 쇼핑 가셨어요.
- 나는 그냥 온라인 쇼핑해.
- 저는 취미로 테니스를 쳐요.
- 저는 요가보다는 필라테스를 선호해요.
- 나는 근육을 만들려고 헬스장에 가.
- 나 결국 오늘 집 전체를 청소했어.
- 난 주말에는 밀린 집안일을 해야 해.
- 저 계속 잘 거예요.

Mom went shopping at the department store. I just shop online. I play tennis as a hobby. I prefer doing pilates to yoga. I go to the gym to build muscle. I finally cleaned the whole house today. I should catch up on housework on weekends. I am going to sleep in.

1st step

QR코드를 통해 음원을 들으며, 그날 배울 영어 표현을 따라 말해보고, 손으로 써보며 익히는 학습의 첫 번째 단계입니다.

2nd step

1st step에서 배운 표현으로 영어 문장을 만들어보며 확인하는 학습의 두 번째 단계입니다. 영어 문장을 만들어보며 문장 속에서 표현이 어떻게 쓰이는지 확인합니다.

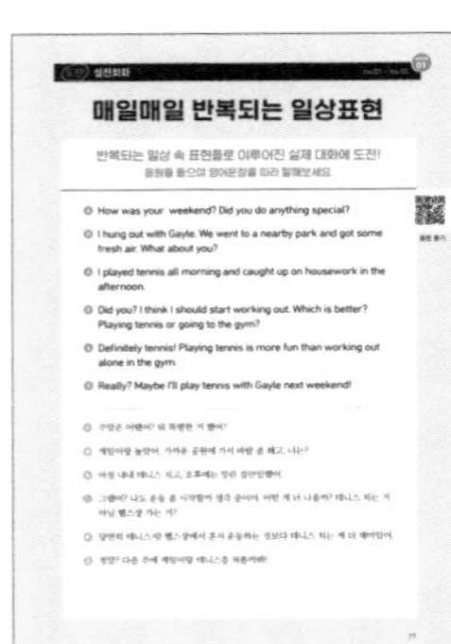
실전회화

매일매일 반복되는 일상표현

반복되는 일상 속 표현들로 이루어진 실제 대화에 도전!
음원을 들으며 영어문장을 따라 말해보세요.

- How was your weekend? Did you do anything special?
- I hung out with Gayle. We went to a nearby park and got some fresh air. What about you?
- I played tennis all morning and caught up on housework in the afternoon.
- Did you? I think I should start working out. Which is better? Playing tennis or going to the gym?
- Definitely tennis! Playing tennis is more fun than working out alone in the gym.
- Really? Maybe I'll play tennis with Gayle next weekend!

도전! **실전회화**

QR코드를 통해 음원을 들으며,
앞에서 배운 표현들로 이루어진
실제 영어대화를 따라 말해봅니다.
영어회화는 입을 많이 뗄수록 실력이 는다는 것!
잊지 마세요.

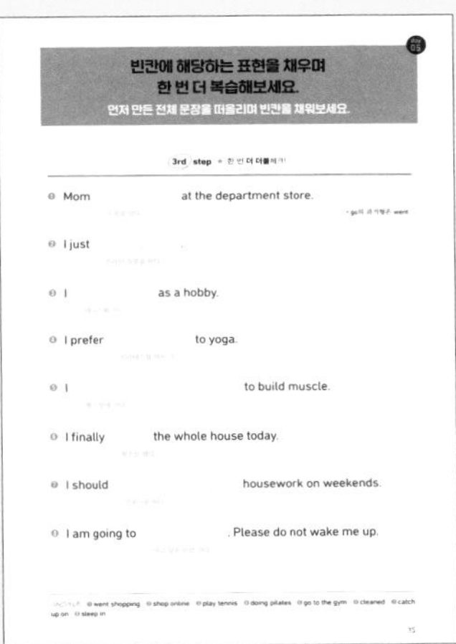

빈칸에 해당하는 표현을 채우며
한 번 더 복습해보세요.
먼저 만든 전체 문장을 떠올리며 빈칸을 채워보세요.

3rd step ∗ 한 번 더 더블체크!

① Mom ______ at the department store.
② I just ______.
③ I ______ as a hobby.
④ I prefer ______ to yoga.
⑤ I ______ to build muscle.
⑥ I finally ______ the whole house today.
⑦ I should ______ housework on weekends.
⑧ I am going to ______. Please do not wake me up.

① went shopping ② shop online ③ play tennis ④ doing pilates ⑤ go to the gym ⑥ cleaned ⑦ catch up on ⑧ sleep in

35

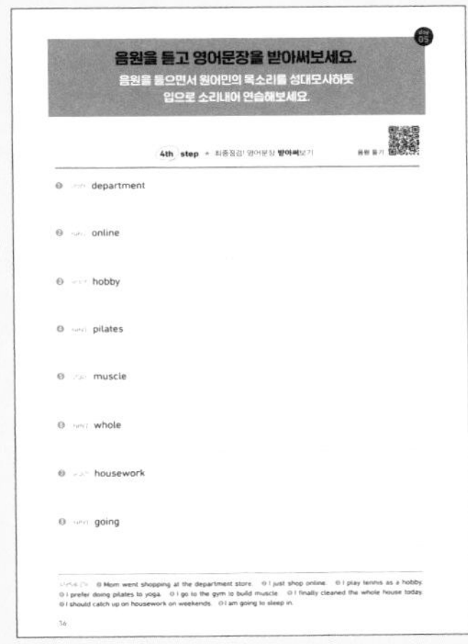

음원을 듣고 영어문장을 받아써보세요.
음원을 들으면서 원어민의 목소리를 성대모사하듯
입으로 소리내어 연습해보세요.

4th step ∗ 최종점검! 영어문장 받아써보기

① department
② online
③ hobby
④ pilates
⑤ muscle
⑥ whole
⑦ housework
⑧ going

① Mom went shopping at the department store. ② I just shop online. ③ I play tennis as a hobby. ④ I prefer doing pilates to yoga. ⑤ I go to the gym to build muscle. ⑥ I finally cleaned the whole house today. ⑦ I should catch up on housework on weekends. ⑧ I am going to sleep in.

36

3rd step

빈칸을 채우며 앞에서 배운 표현을 한번 더 확인하는 학습의 세 번째 단계입니다. 더블체크를 통해 표현을 확실히 내것으로 만들도록 합니다.

4th step

QR코드를 통해 음원을 들으며, 영어 문장을 받아써보는 학습의 네 번째 단계입니다. 음원을 들으며 표현과 문장이 영어로 어떻게 소리나는지 확인하고, 원어민의 목소리를 성대모사하듯 입으로 소리내어 연습하도록 합니다.

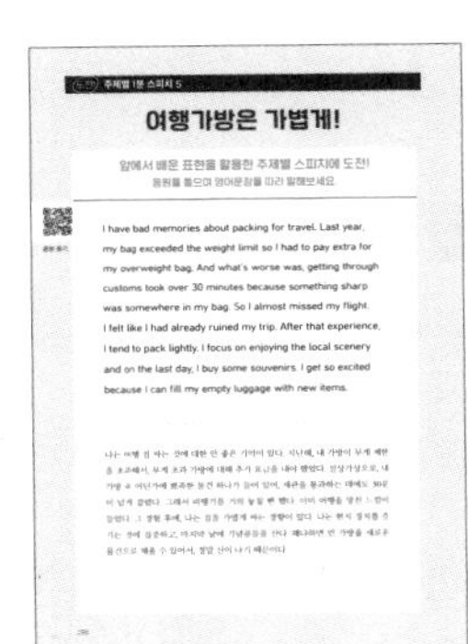

도전! 주제별 1분 스피치 5

여행가방은 가볍게!

앞에서 배운 표현을 활용한 주제별 스피치에 도전!
음원을 들으며 영어문장을 따라 말해보세요.

I have bad memories about packing for travel. Last year, my bag exceeded the weight limit so I had to pay extra for my overweight bag. And what's worse was, getting through customs took over 30 minutes because something sharp was somewhere in my bag. So I almost missed my flight. I felt like I had already ruined my trip. After that experience, I tend to pack lightly. I focus on enjoying the local scenery and on the last day, I buy some souvenirs. I get so excited because I can fill my empty luggage with new items.

도전! **주제별 1분 스피치**

QR코드를 통해 음원을 들으며,
1분 가량의 주제별 스피치에 도전해봅니다.
영어 실력이 업그레이드 되는
스피치 코너를 부록으로 수록하였습니다.

차 례

주제별 필수표현

week 01

매일매일 반복되는 일상표현

week 02

입금은 나의 힘! 출근하기&일하기

week 03

나를 위한 Push-up! 자기계발&문화생활

week 04

먹고 마시고~ 음식&술

week 05

열심히 달린 나를 위한 선물, 쇼핑&여행

week 06

내가 왕년에~~ 지난 시절 이야기

week 07

사람에 대해 설명하기, 습관&성격&외모

week 08

관리가 필요한 것들…
건강 관리&돈 관리&자동차 관리

week 09

대화를 시작하기 좋은 주제들,
스몰토크

week 10

반대가 끌리는 이유! 짝꿍 동사구

기본동사별 필수표현

week 11

이것만 알아도 영어가 쉬워진다! 기본이 되는 핵심 동사들 1

week 12

이것만 알아도 영어가 쉬워진다! 기본이 되는 핵심 동사들 2

도전! 주제별 1분 스피치

주제별 필수표현

week 01

매일매일 반복되는 일상표현

day 01 일상생활 1

매일 아침 반복되는 일상과 관련된 표현입니다.

음원을 듣고 영어표현을 따라 말한 후, 손으로 써보세요.

1st step ★ 따라 **말**하고 **써**보며 표현 **익**히기

음원 듣기

❶ 아침을 간단하게/많이 먹다 ▸ have a light/heavy breakfast

❷ 아침식사를 거르다 ▸ skip breakfast

❸ 집을 나서다 ▸ leave one's place

❹ 버스/지하철을 타다 ▸ take the bus/subway

❺ 운전해서/걸어서 일하러 가다 ▸ drive/walk to work

❻ 버스에서 지하철로 갈아타다 ▸ transfer from bus to subway

❼ 지하철에서 서서 가다 ▸ stand on the subway

❽ 직장에 도착하다 ▸ get to work

day 01

앞에서 배운 표현을 떠올리며 한글에 해당하는 영어문장을 만들어보세요.

전체 문장을 만드는 게 어렵다면 오른쪽 옆 페이지를 참고하세요.

2nd step ★ 문장 속 표현 **확인**하기

❶ 나는 보통 아침을 간단하게 먹어.

❷ 나 오늘은 아침을 걸렀어.

❸ 나는 7시쯤 집을 나섰어.

❹ 제인은 지하철을 타고 등교해.

❺ 운전해서 출근하는 게 더 나아.

❻ 나는 직장에 갈 때 버스에서 지하철로 갈아타야 해.

❼ 나는 북적이는 지하철에서 서서 가는 것을 좋아하지 않아.

❽ 나는 직장에 제시간에 도착했어.

ANSWER ❶ I usually have a light breakfast. ❷ I skipped breakfast this morning. ❸ I left my place at about 7. ❹ Jane takes the subway to school. ❺ It's better to drive to work. ❻ I have to transfer from bus to subway to work. ❼ I don't like standing on crowded subways. ❽ I got to work on time.

빈칸에 해당하는 표현을 채우며 한 번 더 복습해보세요.

먼저 만든 전체 문장을 떠올리며 빈칸을 채워보세요.

3rd step ★ 한 번 **더 더블**체크!

❶ I usually ______ ______ ______ ______.

→ 아침을 간단하게 먹다

❷ I ______ ______ this morning.

→ 아침식사를 걸렀다

• skip의 과거형은 skipped

❸ I ______ ______ ______ at about 7.

→ 집을 나섰다

• leave의 과거형은 left

❹ Jane ______ ______ ______ to school.

→ 버스를 타다

• 3인칭 단수 주어는 동사에 s 붙이기

❺ It's better to ______ ______ ______.

→ 운전해서 일하러 가다

❻ I have to ______ ______ ______ ______ ______ to work.

→ 버스에서 지하철로 갈아타다

❼ I don't like ______ ______ crowded ______.

→ 지하철에서 서서 가는 것

❽ I ______ ______ ______ on time.

→ 직장에 도착했다

ANSWER ❶ have a light breakfast ❷ skipped breakfast ❸ left my place ❹ takes the bus ❺ drive to work ❻ transfer from bus to subway ❼ standing on, subway ❽ got to work

음원을 듣고 영어문장을 받아써보세요.

음원을 들으면서 원어민의 목소리를 성대모사하듯 입으로 소리내어 연습해보세요.

step ★ 최종점검! 영어문장 **받아써**보기

음원 듣기 

❶ HINT usually

❷ HINT skipped

❸ HINT my, at

❹ HINT to, school

❺ HINT better

❻ HINT transfer, subway

❼ HINT standing, crowded

❽ HINT on, time

ANSWER ❶ I usually have a light breakfast. ❷ I skipped breakfast this morning. ❸ I left my place at about 7. ❹ Jane takes the subway to school. ❺ It's better to drive to work. ❻ I have to transfer from bus to subway to work. ❼ I don't like standing on crowded subways. ❽ I got to work on time.

day 02 일상생활 2

일상생활에서 자주 사용되는 표현입니다.

음원을 듣고 영어표현을 따라 말한 후, 손으로 써보세요.

1st step ★ 따라 **말**하고 **써**보며 표현 **익**히기

음원 듣기

❶ ~와 잘 지내다 ▸ get along with+사람

❷ 바람을 쐬다 ▸ get some fresh air

❸ 회식하다 ▸ have a company dinner

❹ 야근하다 ▸ work overtime

❺ 퇴근하다 ▸ leave the office

❻ 야식을 먹다 ▸ have a late night snack

❼ 잠자리에 들다 ▸ go to bed

❽ 늦게 자다[밤 새다] ▸ stay up late[all night]

앞에서 배운 표현을 떠올리며 한글에 해당하는 영어문장을 만들어보세요.

전체 문장을 만드는 게 어렵다면 오른쪽 옆 페이지를 참고하세요.

2nd step ★ 문장 속 표현 **확인**하기

❶ 사라는 그녀의 동료들과 잘 지내.

❷ 나는 종종 가까운 공원에 가서 바람을 쐐.

❸ 나 이번 주 금요일에 회식이 있어.

❹ 요즘 우리 팀은 자주 야근해.

❺ 나 오늘은 일찍 퇴근할 수 있어.

❻ 나는 요즘 밤마다 야식을 먹어.

❼ 나는 주로 일찍 잠자리에 들어.

❽ 우리 가족은 주로 늦게 자.

ANSWER ❶ Sara gets along with her coworkers. ❷ I often go to a nearby park to get some fresh air. ❸ I have a company dinner this Friday. ❹ These days, my team often works overtime. ❺ I can leave the office early today. ❻ These days, I have a late night snack every night. ❼ I usually go to bed early. ❽ My family usually stays up late.

빈칸에 해당하는 표현을 채우며 한 번 더 복습해보세요.

먼저 만든 전체 문장을 떠올리며 빈칸을 채워보세요.

3rd step ★ 한 번 **더 더블**체크!

❶ Sara ________ her coworkers.
→ ~와 잘 지내다
• 3인칭 단수 주어는 동사에 s 붙이기

❷ I often go to a nearby park to ________ .
→ 바람을 쐬다

❸ I ________ this Friday.
→ 회식하다

❹ These days, my team often ________ .
→ 야근하다
• 3인칭 단수 주어는 동사에 s 붙이기

❺ I can ________ early today.
→ 퇴근하다

❻ These days, I ________ every night.
→ 야식을 먹다

❼ I usually ________ early.
→ 잠자리에 들다

❽ My family usually ________ .
→ 늦게 자다
• 3인칭 단수 주어는 동사에 s 붙이기

ANSWER ❶ gets along with ❷ get some fresh air ❸ have a company dinner ❹ works overtime ❺ leave the office ❻ have a late night snack ❼ go to bed ❽ stays up late

음원을 듣고 영어문장을 받아써보세요.

음원을 들으면서 원어민의 목소리를 성대모사하듯 입으로 소리내어 연습해보세요.

음원 듣기

4th step ★ 최종점검! 영어문장 **받아써**보기

❶ HINT coworkers

❷ HINT nearby

❸ HINT Friday

❹ HINT These, days

❺ HINT office

❻ HINT snack

❼ HINT early

❽ HINT usually

ANSWER ❶ Sara gets along with her coworkers. ❷ I often go to a nearby park to get some fresh air. ❸ I have a company dinner this Friday. ❹ These days, my team often works overtime. ❺ I can leave the office early today. ❻ These days, I have a late night snack every night. ❼ I usually go to bed early. ❽ My family usually stays up late.

집안일

장 보기, 청소하기 등 집안일과 관련된 표현입니다.

음원을 듣고 영어표현을 따라 말한 후, 손으로 써보세요.

1st step ★ 따라 **말**하고 **써**보며 표현 **익**히기

음원 듣기

❶ 집안일하다 ▶ do chores

❷ 어지른 것을 치우다 ▶ clean (up) the mess

❸ 방을 정리하다 ▶ tidy the room

❹ 장 보러 가다 ▶ go grocery shopping

❺ 반찬을 만들다 ▶ make some side dishes

❻ 진공청소기를 돌리다 ▶ vacuum (the floor)

❼ 남은 음식을 냉장고에 넣다 ▶ put the leftovers in the fridge

❽ 분리수거하다 ▶ separate the garbage

앞에서 배운 표현을 떠올리며 한글에 해당하는 영어문장을 만들어보세요.

전체 문장을 만드는 게 어렵다면 오른쪽 옆 페이지를 참고하세요.

2nd step ★ 문장 속 표현 **확인**하기

❶ 나는 주말엔 많은 시간을 집안일을 하느라 보내.

❷ 제발 네가 어질러 놓은 것은 네가 치워.

❸ 방이 어지러워서 내가 치웠어.

❹ 너희 가족 중에 누가 주로 장을 보러 가?

❺ 내가 반찬 몇 개 만들어놨어.

❻ 밤에 청소기 돌리는 것은 허용되지 않아요.

❼ 남은 음식은 냉장고에 넣어둬.

❽ 내 남편이 주로 분리수거를 해.

ANSWER ❶ I spend a lot of time doing chores on the weekend. ❷ Please clean up the mess you made. ❸ The room was untidy so I tidied it. ❹ Who usually goes grocery shopping in your family? ❺ I made some side dishes. ❻ Vacuuming is not allowed at night. ❼ Put the leftovers in the fridge. ❽ My husband usually separates the garbage.

빈칸에 해당하는 표현을 채우며 한 번 더 복습해보세요.

먼저 만든 전체 문장을 떠올리며 빈칸을 채워보세요.

3rd step ★ 한 번 **더 더블**체크!

❶ I spend a lot of time ______ ______ on the weekend.
→ 집안일하는 것

❷ Please ______ ______ ______ ______ you made.
→ 어지른 것을 치우다

❸ The room was untidy so I ______ it.
→ 방을 정리했다
• tidy의 과거형은 tidied

❹ Who usually ______ ______ ______ in your family?
→ 장 보러 가다
• 3인칭 단수 주어에는 주어에 (e)s 붙이기

❺ I ______ ______ ______ ______.
→ 반찬을 좀 만들었다
• make의 과거형은 made

❻ ______ is not allowed at night.
→ 청소기를 돌리는 것

❼ ______ ______ ______ ______ ______ ______.
→ 남은 음식을 냉장고에 넣다

❽ My husband usually ______ ______ ______.
→ 분리수거하다
• 3인칭 단수 주어는 동사에 s 붙이기

ANSWER ❶ doing chores ❷ clean up the mess ❸ tidied ❹ goes grocery shopping ❺ made some side dishes ❻ Vacuuming ❼ Put the leftovers in the fridge ❽ separates the garbage

음원을 듣고 영어문장을 받아써보세요.

음원을 들으면서 원어민의 목소리를 성대모사하듯 입으로 소리내어 연습해보세요.

4th step ★ 최종점검! 영어문장 **받아써**보기

음원 듣기

❶ HINT chores

❷ HINT mess

❸ HINT untidy

❹ HINT grocery

❺ HINT dishes

❻ HINT allowed

❼ HINT leftovers, fridge

❽ HINT garbage

ANSWER ❶ I spend a lot of time doing chores on the weekend. ❷ Please clean up the mess you made. ❸ The room was untidy so I tidied it. ❹ Who usually goes grocery shopping in your family? ❺ I made some side dishes. ❻ Vacuuming is not allowed at night. ❼ Put the leftovers in the fridge. ❽ My husband usually separates the garbage.

취미생활과 주말 1

재충전에 꼭 필요한 취미생활과 주말에 관련된 표현입니다.

음원을 듣고 영어표현을 따라 말한 후, 손으로 써보세요.

1st step ★ 따라 **말**하고 **써**보며 표현 **익**히기

음원 듣기

❶ 취미가 있다 ▸ have some hobbies

❷ 영화를 보다 ▸ watch movies

❸ 가까운 공원에 가다 ▸ go to a nearby park

❹ 영어학원에 가다 ▸ go to the English academy

❺ 자전거를 타다 ▸ ride a bicycle

❻ 강아지를 산책시키다 ▸ take a walk with one's dog

❼ 친구들과 놀다 ▸ hang out with friends

❽ 데이트하러 가다 ▸ go on a date

앞에서 배운 표현을 떠올리며 한글에 해당하는 영어문장을 만들어보세요.

전체 문장을 만드는 게 어렵다면 오른쪽 옆 페이지를 참고하세요.

2nd step ★ 문장 속 표현 **확인**하기

❶ 지금은 특별한 취미가 없어요.

❷ 영어자막만으로 영화를 보는 건 어때?

❸ 나는 가까운 공원에 가서 산책해.

❹ 저는 주말마다 영어학원에 가요.

❺ 나는 한강을 따라 자전거 타는 걸 좋아해.

❻ 최소 일주일에 한 번은 강아지를 산책시키려고 노력해요.

❼ 저는 친구들과 놀면서 스트레스를 풀어요.

❽ 나는 주말엔 보통 남자친구와 데이트해.

ANSWER ❶ I don't have any special hobbies for now. ❷ How about watching movies only with English subtitles? ❸ I go to a nearby park and walk around. ❹ I go to the English academy every weekend. ❺ I like to ride a bicycle along the Han river. ❻ I try to take a walk with my dog at least once a week. ❼ I relieve stress by hanging out with my friends. ❽ I usually go on a date with my boyfriend on the weekend.

빈칸에 해당하는 표현을 채우며 한 번 더 복습해보세요.

먼저 만든 전체 문장을 떠올리며 빈칸을 채워보세요.

3rd step ★ 한 번 **더 더블**체크!

❶ I don't ________ special ________ for now.
→ 취미가 있다
• some은 부정문에서 any로 쓰임

❷ How about ________ only with English subtitles?
→ 영화를 보는 것

❸ I ________ and walk around.
→ 가까운 공원에 가다

❹ I ________ every weekend.
→ 영어학원에 가다

❺ I like to ________ along the Han river.
→ 자전거를 타다

❻ I try to ________ at least once a week.
→ 강아지를 산책시키다

❼ I relieve stress by ________ my ________.
→ 친구들과 노는 것

❽ I usually ________ with my boyfriend on the weekend.
→ 데이트하러 가다

ANSWER ❶ have any, hobbies ❷ watching movies ❸ go to a nearby park ❹ go to the English academy ❺ ride a bicycle ❻ take a walk with my dog ❼ hanging out with, friends ❽ go on a date

음원을 듣고 영어문장을 받아써보세요.

음원을 들으면서 원어민의 목소리를 성대모사하듯
입으로 소리내어 연습해보세요.

 step ★ 최종점검! 영어문장 **받아써**보기 음원 듣기

❶ HINT for, now

❷ HINT subtitles

❸ HINT nearby

❹ HINT weekend

❺ HINT along

❻ HINT at, least

❼ HINT relieve

❽ HINT usually

ANSWER ❶ I don't have any special hobbies for now. ❷ How about watching movies only with English subtitles? ❸ I go to a nearby park and walk around. ❹ I go to the English academy every weekend. ❺ I like to ride a bicycle along the Han river. ❻ I try to take a walk with my dog at least once a week. ❼ I relieve stress by hanging out with my friends. ❽ I usually go on a date with my boyfriend on the weekend.

취미생활과 주말 2

운동, 쇼핑 등 취미생활과 주말에 관련된 표현입니다.

음원을 듣고 영어표현을 따라 말한 후, 손으로 써보세요.

1st step ★ 따라 **말**하고 **써**보며 표현 **익**히기

음원 듣기

❶ 쇼핑을 가다 ▶ go shopping

❷ 온라인 쇼핑을 하다 ▶ shop online

❸ 테니스를 치다 ▶ play tennis

❹ 요가/필라테스를 하다 ▶ do yoga/pilates

❺ 헬스장에 가다 ▶ go to the gym

❻ 청소를 하다 ▶ clean+공간

❼ 밀린 ~을 하다 ▶ catch up on ~

❽ 자고 싶은 만큼 자다 ▶ sleep in

앞에서 배운 표현을 떠올리며 한글에 해당하는 영어문장을 만들어보세요.

전체 문장을 만드는 게 어렵다면 오른쪽 옆 페이지를 참고하세요.

2nd step ★ 문장 속 표현 **확인**하기

❶ 엄마는 백화점으로 쇼핑 가셨어요.

❷ 나는 그냥 온라인 쇼핑해.

❸ 저는 취미로 테니스를 쳐요.

❹ 저는 요가보다는 필라테스를 선호해요.

❺ 나는 근육을 만들려고 헬스장에 가.

❻ 나 결국 오늘 집 전체를 청소했어.

❼ 난 주말에는 밀린 집안일을 해야 해.

❽ 저 계속 잘 거예요.

ANSWER ❶ Mom went shopping at the department store. ❷ I just shop online. ❸ I play tennis as a hobby. ❹ I prefer doing pilates to yoga. ❺ I go to the gym to build muscle. ❻ I finally cleaned the whole house today. ❼ I should catch up on housework on weekends. ❽ I am going to sleep in.

빈칸에 해당하는 표현을 채우며 한 번 더 복습해보세요.

먼저 만든 전체 문장을 떠올리며 빈칸을 채워보세요.

3rd step ★ 한 번 **더 더블**체크!

❶ Mom ________ ________ at the department store.

→ 쇼핑을 갔다

• go의 과거형은 went

❷ I just ________ ________ .

→ 온라인 쇼핑을 하다

❸ I ________ ________ as a hobby.

→ 테니스를 치다

❹ I prefer ________ ________ to yoga.

→ 필라테스를 하는 것

❺ I ________ ________ ________ ________ to build muscle.

→ 헬스장에 가다

❻ I finally ________ the whole house today.

→ 청소를 했다

❼ I should ________ ________ ________ housework on weekends.

→ 밀린 ~을 하다

❽ I am going to ________ ________ .

→ 자고 싶은 만큼 자다

ANSWER ❶ went shopping ❷ shop online ❸ play tennis ❹ doing pilates ❺ go to the gym ❻ cleaned ❼ catch up on ❽ sleep in

음원을 듣고 영어문장을 받아써보세요.

음원을 들으면서 원어민의 목소리를 성대모사하듯 입으로 소리내어 연습해보세요.

step ★ 최종점검! 영어문장 **받아써**보기

음원 듣기 

❶ HINT department

❷ HINT online

❸ HINT hobby

❹ HINT pilates

❺ HINT muscle

❻ HINT whole

❼ HINT housework

❽ HINT going

ANSWER ❶ Mom went shopping at the department store. ❷ I just shop online. ❸ I play tennis as a hobby. ❹ I prefer doing pilates to yoga. ❺ I go to the gym to build muscle. ❻ I finally cleaned the whole house today. ❼ I should catch up on housework on weekends. ❽ I am going to sleep in.

매일매일 반복되는 일상표현

반복되는 일상 속 표현들로 이루어진 실제 대화에 도전!
음원을 들으며 영어문장을 따라 말해보세요.

음원 듣기

Ⓐ How was your weekend? Did you do anything special?

Ⓑ I hung out with Gayle. We went to a nearby park and got some fresh air. What about you?

Ⓐ I played tennis all morning and caught up on housework in the afternoon.

Ⓑ Did you? I think I should start working out. Which is better? Playing tennis or going to the gym?

Ⓐ Definitely tennis! Playing tennis is more fun than working out alone in the gym.

Ⓑ Really? Maybe I'll play tennis with Gayle next weekend!

Ⓐ 주말은 어땠어? 뭐 특별한 거 했어?

Ⓑ 게일이랑 놀았어. 가까운 공원에 가서 바람 좀 쐐고. 너는?

Ⓐ 아침 내내 테니스 치고, 오후에는 밀린 집안일했어.

Ⓑ 그랬어? 나도 운동 좀 시작할까 생각 중이야. 어떤 게 더 나을까? 테니스 치는 거 아님 헬스장 가는 거?

Ⓐ 당연히 테니스지! 헬스장에서 혼자 운동하는 것보다 테니스 치는 게 더 재미있어.

Ⓑ 정말? 다음 주에 게일이랑 테니스를 쳐볼까봐!

week 02

입금은 나의 힘!
출근하기&일하기

day 06 직장생활 1

day 07 직장생활 2

day 08 직장생활 3

day 09 직장생활 4

day 10 외국인과 통화하기

day 06 직장생활 1

하루 중 가장 많은 시간을 보내는 곳인 직장생활과 관련된 표현입니다.

음원을 듣고 영어표현을 따라 말한 후, 손으로 써보세요.

1st step ★ 따라 **말**하고 **써**보며 표현 **익**히기

음원 듣기

❶ 낮/밤 근무를 하다 ▸ work the day/night shift

❷ 지하철로 통근하다 ▸ commute by subway

❸ 외근 나가다 ▸ work outside of the office

❹ 하루 쉬다, 월차 내다 ▸ take a day off

❺ 며칠 쉬다 ▸ take a few days off

❻ 주말에 일하다 ▸ work on the weekend

❼ 근무시간이 자유롭다 ▸ have a flexible schedule

❽ ~에 익숙하다[익숙해졌다] ▸ be[got] used to -ing

day 06

앞에서 배운 표현을 떠올리며 한글에 해당하는 영어문장을 만들어보세요.

전체 문장을 만드는 게 어렵다면 오른쪽 옆 페이지를 참고하세요.

2nd step ★ 문장 속 표현 **확인**하기

❶ 오늘은 저녁 근무를 해요.

❷ 저는 주로 지하철로 통근해요.

❸ 저 오늘은 외근 나가요.

❹ 저 다음 주에 하루 쉴 거예요.

❺ 며칠 월차 내고 일본 여행했어요.

❻ 네가 주말마다 일하면, 우리는 언제 데이트해?

❼ 저는 근무시간이 자유로운 게 좋아요.

❽ 지금은 일에 익숙해져서, 제시간에 퇴근해요.

ANSWER ❶ I work the night shift today. ❷ I usually commute by subway. ❸ I work outside of the office today. ❹ I will take a day off next week. ❺ I took a few days off and traveled to Japan. ❻ If you work on the weekend, when can we go out on a date? ❼ I like to have a flexible schedule. ❽ Now I am used to the work, so I leave the office on time.

빈칸에 해당하는 표현을 채우며 한 번 더 복습해보세요.

먼저 만든 전체 문장을 떠올리며 빈칸을 채워보세요.

3rd step ★ 한 번 **더 더블**체크!

❶ I ______________ today.
→ 밤 근무를 하다

❷ I usually ______________ .
→ 지하철로 통근하다

❸ I ______________ today.
→ 외근 나가다

❹ I will ______________ next week.
→ 월차 내다

❺ I ______________ and traveled to Japan.
→ 며칠 쉬다

• take의 과거형은 took

❻ If you ______________ , when can we go out on a date?
→ 주말에 일하다

❼ I like to ______________ .
→ 근무시간이 자유롭다

❽ Now I ______________ the work, so I leave the office on time.
→ ~에 익숙하다

ANSWER ❶ work the night shift ❷ commute by subway ❸ work outside of the office ❹ take a day off ❺ took a few days off ❻ work on the weekend ❼ have a flexible schedule ❽ am used to

음원을 듣고 영어문장을 받아써보세요.

음원을 들으면서 원어민의 목소리를 성대모사하듯 입으로 소리내어 연습해보세요.

음원 듣기

4th step ★ 최종점검! 영어문장 **받아써**보기

❶ HINT shift

❷ HINT commute

❸ HINT outside

❹ HINT will

❺ HINT traveled, to

❻ HINT go, out

❼ HINT flexible, schedule

❽ HINT on, time

ANSWER ❶ I work the night shift today. ❷ I usually commute by subway. ❸ I work outside of the office today. ❹ I will take a day off next week. ❺ I took a few days off and traveled to Japan. ❻ If you work on the weekend, when can we go out on a date? ❼ I like to have a flexible schedule. ❽ Now I am used to the work, so I leave the office on time.

day 07 직장생활 2

미팅, 출장, 동료들과의 관계 등
직장생활과 관련된 표현입니다.

음원을 듣고 영어표현을 따라 말한 후, 손으로 써보세요.

1st step ★ 따라 **말**하고 **써**보며 표현 **익**히기

음원 듣기

1. 고객과 만나다 ▶ meet with clients
2. 상사와 토의하다 ▶ talk with one's supervisor
3. 동료들과 (의견충돌로) 다투다 ▶ argue with one's coworkers
4. 동료들과 잘 지내다 ▶ get along with one's coworkers
5. 출장을 가다 ▶ go on a business trip
6. 병가를 내다 ▶ take sick leave
7. 일을 그만두다 ▶ quit one's job
8. 해고되다 ▶ get fired

앞에서 배운 표현을 떠올리며 한글에 해당하는 영어문장을 만들어보세요.

전체 문장을 만드는 게 어렵다면 오른쪽 옆 페이지를 참고하세요.

2nd step ★ 문장 속 표현 **확인**하기

❶ 저는 고객들과 5시에 미팅이 있어요.

❷ 저는 상사와 대화를 할 때는 불안해요.

❸ 그 회의에서 동료와 의견 충돌이 좀 있었어요.

❹ 저는 동료들과 잘 지내는 편이에요.

❺ 다음 주에 일본으로 출장을 가요.

❻ 저 병가를 내야 할 것 같아요.

❼ 일을 그만두고 어딘가로 가고 싶어.

❽ 요즘은 해고될까 두려워.

ANSWER ❶ I'm meeting with my client at 5. ❷ I get nervous when I talk with my supervisor. ❸ I argued with my coworker at the meeting. ❹ I tend to get along with my coworkers. ❺ I'm going on a business trip to Japan next week. ❻ I think I should take sick leave. ❼ I want to quit my job and go somewhere. ❽ I am afraid of getting fired.

빈칸에 해당하는 표현을 채우며 한 번 더 복습해보세요.

먼저 만든 전체 문장을 떠올리며 빈칸을 채워보세요.

3rd step ★ 한 번 **더 더블**체크!

❶ I'm ______ my ______ at 5.
→ 고객들과 만나다
• be -ing로 가까운 미래를 나타냄

❷ I get nervous when I ______ .
→ 상사와 이야기하다

❸ I ______ at the meeting.
→ 동료와 다퉜다

❹ I tend to ______ .
→ 동료들과 잘 지내다

❺ I'm ______ to Japan next week.
→ 출장을 가다
• be -ing로 가까운 미래를 나타냄

❻ I think I should ______ .
→ 병가를 내다

❼ I want to ______ and go somewhere.
→ 일을 그만두다

❽ I am afraid of ______ .
→ 해고되는 것

ANSWER ❶ meeting with, clients ❷ talk with my supervisor ❸ argued with my coworker ❹ get along with my coworkers ❺ going on a business trip ❻ take sick leave ❼ quit my job ❽ getting fired

음원을 듣고 영어문장을 받아써보세요.

음원을 들으면서 원어민의 목소리를 성대모사하듯 입으로 소리내어 연습해보세요.

음원 듣기

4th step ★ 최종점검! 영어문장 **받아써**보기

❶ HINT client

❷ HINT nervous, supervisor

❸ HINT argued

❹ HINT tend

❺ HINT Japan

❻ HINT should

❼ HINT somewhere

❽ HINT afraid

ANSWER ❶ I'm meeting with my client at 5. ❷ I get nervous when I talk with my supervisor. ❸ I argued with my coworker at the meeting. ❹ I tend to get along with my coworkers. ❺ I'm going on a business trip to Japan next week. ❻ I think I should take sick leave. ❼ I want to quit my job and go somewhere. ❽ I am afraid of getting fired.

day 08 직장생활 3

승진, 월급, 이직 등
직장생활과 관련된 표현입니다.

음원을 듣고 영어표현을 따라 말한 후, 손으로 써보세요.

1st step ★ 따라 **말**하고 **써**보며 표현 **익**히기

음원 듣기

1. 승진하다 ▸ get promoted
2. 월급을 받다 ▸ get paid
3. 월급인상을 받다 ▸ get a raise
4. 보너스를 받다 ▸ get a bonus
5. 이직하다 ▸ transfer to another company
6. 은퇴를 하다 ▸ retire (from the company)
7. 좋은 직장을 가지다 ▸ have a good job
8. 더 좋은 직장을 얻다 ▸ get a better job

앞에서 배운 표현을 떠올리며 한글에 해당하는 영어문장을 만들어보세요.

전체 문장을 만드는 게 어렵다면 오른쪽 옆 페이지를 참고하세요.

2nd step ★ 문장 속 표현 **확인**하기

❶ 너는 승진할 자격이 있어.

❷ 나는 매달 10일에 월급을 받아.

❸ 나는 월급인상을 받을 자격이 있어.

❹ 보너스 많이 받는 팁 좀 알려주세요.

❺ 나 곧 다른 회사로 이직할 계획이야.

❻ 어머니는 30년 근무 후 은퇴하셨다.

❼ 좋은 직장을 가진다는 것의 의미가 뭘까?

❽ 나는 내 미래를 위해서 더 좋은 직장을 얻으려고 노력하고 있어.

ANSWER ❶ You deserve to get promoted. ❷ I get paid on the 10th of every month. ❸ I deserve to get a raise. ❹ Give me some tips on how to get a big bonus. ❺ I am planning to transfer to another company soon. ❻ My mother retired after 30 years of work. ❼ What does it mean to have a good job? ❽ I am trying to get a better job for my future.

빈칸에 해당하는 표현을 채우며 한 번 더 복습해보세요.

먼저 만든 전체 문장을 떠올리며 빈칸을 채워보세요.

3rd step ★ 한 번 **더 더블**체크!

❶ You deserve to ______ ______ .
→ 승진하다

❷ I ______ ______ on the 10th of every month.
→ 월급을 받다

❸ I deserve to ______ ______ ______ .
→ 월급인상을 받다

❹ Give me some tips on how to ______ ______ big ______ .
→ 보너스를 받다

❺ I am planning to ______ ______ ______ ______ soon.
→ 이직하다

❻ My mother ______ after 30 years of work.
→ 은퇴했다

❼ What does it mean to ______ ______ ______ ______ ?
→ 좋은 직장을 가지다

❽ I am trying to ______ ______ ______ ______ for my future.
→ 더 좋은 직장을 얻다

ANSWER ❶ get promoted ❷ get paid ❸ get a raise ❹ get a, bonus ❺ transfer to another company ❻ retired ❼ have a good job ❽ get a better job

음원을 듣고 영어문장을 받아써보세요.

음원을 들으면서 원어민의 목소리를 성대모사하듯 입으로 소리내어 연습해보세요.

4th step ★ 최종점검! 영어문장 **받아써**보기

음원 듣기

❶ HINT deserve

❷ HINT the, 10th

❸ HINT raise

❹ HINT tips, big

❺ HINT planning

❻ HINT retired

❼ HINT mean

❽ HINT better

ANSWER ❶ You deserve to get promoted. ❷ I get paid on the 10th of every month. ❸ I deserve to get a raise. ❹ Give me some tips on how to get a big bonus. ❺ I am planning to transfer to another company soon. ❻ My mother retired after 30 years of work. ❼ What does it mean to have a good job? ❽ I am trying to get a better job for my future.

day 09 직장생활 4

**경력, 근무시간, 근무 형태 등
직장생활과 관련된 표현입니다.**

음원을 듣고 영어표현을 따라 말한 후, 손으로 써보세요.

1st step ★ 따라 **말**하고 **써**보며 표현 **익**히기

❶ 
안정적인 직업을 가지다 ▸ get a stable job

❷ 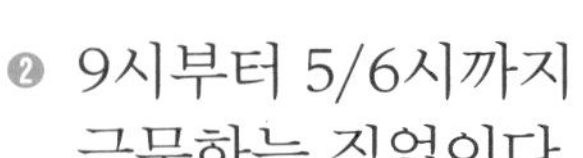
9시부터 5/6시까지 근무하는 직업이다 ▸ have a 9 to 5/6 job

❸ 급여가 높은 직업을 가지다 ▸ have a high paying job

❹ 급여가 낮은 직업을 가지다 ▸ have a low paying job

❺ 정규직이다(정규직을 갖다) ▸ have a regular job

❻ 비정규직이다(비정규직을 갖다) ▸ have a non-regular job

❼ 공무원이다(정부를 위해 일하다) ▸ work for the government

❽ 경력을 쌓다 ▸ gain work experience

앞에서 배운 표현을 떠올리며 한글에 해당하는 영어문장을 만들어보세요.

전체 문장을 만드는 게 어렵다면 오른쪽 옆 페이지를 참고하세요.

2nd step ★ 문장 속 표현 **확인**하기

❶ 요즘 안정적인 직장을 가지는 것은 어려워.

❷ 나는 9시부터 5시까지 일하는 직업을 가지고 있어.

❸ 나는 급여가 높은 직업을 갖는다면 행복할 거야.

❹ 급여가 낮은 직업이지만 나는 그 일을 좋아해.

❺ 이건 내 첫 정규직 직업이야.

❻ 비정규직에 대한 사회 문제들이 있어.

❼ 우리 아버지는 공무원이셔.

❽ 나는 경력을 더 쌓아서 급여가 나은 곳으로 이직하고 싶어.

ANSWER ❶ It's difficult to get a stable job these days. ❷ I have a 9 to 5 job. ❸ I would be happy if I had a high paying job. ❹ I have a low paying job but I like the work. ❺ It is my first regular job. ❻ There are social issues about non-regular jobs. ❼ My father works for the government. ❽ I'd like to gain more work experience and transfer to another company that pays better.

빈칸에 해당하는 표현을 채우며 한 번 더 복습해보세요.

먼저 만든 전체 문장을 떠올리며 빈칸을 채워보세요.

3rd step ★ 한 번 **더 더블**체크!

❶ It's difficult to ______ ______ ______ ______ these days.
→ 안정적인 직업을 가지다

❷ I ______ ______ ______ ______ ______ ______ .
→ 9시부터 5시까지 근무하는 직업이다

❸ I would be happy if I ______ ______ ______ ______ ______ .
→ 급여가 높은 직업을 가졌다
• have의 과거형은 had

❹ I ______ ______ ______ ______ ______ but I like the work.
→ 급여가 낮은 직업을 가지다

❺ It is my first ______ ______ .
→ 정규직

❻ There are social issues about ______ ______ .
→ 비정규직들

❼ My father ______ ______ ______ ______ .
→ 공무원이다
• 3인칭 단수 주어는 동사에 s 붙이기

❽ I'd like to ______ more ______ ______ and transfer to another company that pays better.
→ 경력을 쌓다

ANSWER ❶ get a stable job ❷ have a 9 to 5 job ❸ had a high paying job ❹ have a low paying job ❺ regular job ❻ non-regular jobs ❼ works for the government ❽ gain, work experience

음원을 듣고 영어문장을 받아써보세요.

음원을 들으면서 원어민의 목소리를 성대모사하듯
입으로 소리내어 연습해보세요.

4th step ★ 최종점검! 영어문장 **받아써**보기 음원 듣기

❶ HINT stable

❷ HINT to

❸ HINT would

❹ HINT work

❺ HINT regular

❻ HINT social, issues

❼ HINT government

❽ HINT gain, transfer

ANSWER ❶ It's difficult to get a stable job these days. ❷ I have a 9 to 5 job. ❸ I would be happy if I had a high paying job. ❹ I have a low paying job but I like the work. ❺ It is my first regular job. ❻ There are social issues about non-regular jobs. ❼ My father works for the government. ❽ I'd like to gain more work experience and transfer to another company that pays better.

day 10 외국인과 통화하기

직장에서 겪을 수 있는 외국인과의 전화통화와 관련된 표현입니다.

음원을 듣고 영어표현을 따라 말한 후, 손으로 써보세요.

1st step ★ 따라 **말**하고 **써**보며 표현 **익**히기

음원 듣기

❶ ~와 통화하다 ▶ speak to ~

❷ 메시지를 남기다 ▶ leave a message

❸ 통화 중이다 ▶ be on another line

❹ 잘못 걸다 ▶ get the wrong number

❺ 반복해서 말하다 ▶ repeat

❻ 크게 말하다 ▶ speak up

❼ 천천히 말하다 ▶ slow down

❽ 철자를 말하다 ▶ spell

앞에서 배운 표현을 떠올리며 한글에 해당하는 영어문장을 만들어보세요.

전체 문장을 만드는 게 어렵다면 오른쪽 옆 페이지를 참고하세요.

2nd step ★ 문장 속 표현 **확인**하기

❶ 게일과 통화할 수 있을까요?

❷ 그에게 메시지를 남길 수 있을까요?

❸ 죄송합니다만 그는 지금 통화 중입니다.

❹ 잘못 거신 것 같습니다.

❺ 못 알아들었는데, 다시 말씀해주시겠어요?

❻ 잘 안 들리는데, 좀 더 크게 말씀해주시겠어요?

❼ 조금만 천천히 말씀해주시겠어요?

❽ 철자를 말씀해주시겠습니까?

ANSWER ❶ Could I speak to Gayle? ❷ Could I leave a message for him? ❸ I'm afraid he's on another line. ❹ I think you've got the wrong number. ❺ I don't understand. Could you repeat that? ❻ I can't hear you very well. Could you speak up a little? ❼ Could you slow down a bit? ❽ Could you spell that, please?

day 10

빈칸에 해당하는 표현을 채우며 한 번 더 복습해보세요.

먼저 만든 전체 문장을 떠올리며 빈칸을 채워보세요.

3rd step ★ 한 번 **더 더블**체크!

❶ Could I ______________ Gayle?
→ ~와 통화하다

❷ Could I ______________ for him?
→ 메시지를 남기다

❸ I'm afraid he's ______________.
→ 통화 중이다

❹ I think you've ______________.
→ 잘못 걸었다

❺ I don't understand. Could you ______________ that?
→ 반복해서 말하다

❻ I can't hear you very well. Could you ______________ a little?
→ 크게 말하다

❼ Could you ______________ a bit?
→ 천천히 말하다

❽ Could you ______________ that, please?
→ 철자를 말하다

ANSWER ❶ speak to ❷ leave a message ❸ on another line ❹ got the wrong number ❺ repeat ❻ speak up ❼ slow down ❽ spell

음원을 듣고 영어문장을 받아써보세요.

음원을 들으면서 원어민의 목소리를 성대모사하듯 입으로 소리내어 연습해보세요.

4th step ★ 최종점검! 영어문장 **받아써**보기

음원 듣기 

❶ HINT Could

❷ HINT message

❸ HINT on, another

❹ HINT you've, wrong

❺ HINT repeat

❻ HINT hear

❼ HINT a, bit

❽ HINT spell

ANSWER ❶ Could I speak to Gayle? ❷ Could I leave a message for him? ❸ I'm afraid he's on another line. ❹ I think you've got the wrong number. ❺ I don't understand. Could you repeat that? ❻ I can't hear you very well. Could you speak up a little? ❼ Could you slow down a bit? ❽ Could you spell that, please?

입금은 나의 힘! 출근하기&일하기

직장에서 빈번히 일어나는 표현들로 이루어진 실제 대화에 도전!
음원을 들으며 영어문장을 따라 말해보세요.

음원 듣기

Ⓐ How's your new job? Are you getting used to it?

Ⓑ I think so. I am getting along with my new coworkers, too. They are really nice.

Ⓐ You made the right decision with transferring to that company.

Ⓑ That's right, plus I can get a raise when I gain enough work experience.

Ⓐ I'm sure you will do well at your new job.

Ⓑ Thank you so much! I'll talk to you later. I'm meeting with my client at 3.

Ⓐ 새로운 일은 어때요? 익숙해지고 있는 중이에요?

Ⓑ 그런 것 같아요. 새 동료들과도 잘 어울리고 있고요. 그들은 정말 친절해요.

Ⓐ 그 회사로 이직한 거 결정을 잘했네요.

Ⓑ 맞아요. 게다가 충분한 경력을 쌓으면 임금인상도 받을 수 있고요.

Ⓐ 당신 새 직장에서 잘할 거예요.

Ⓑ 정말 고마워요! 나중에 얘기해요. 제가 고객과 3시에 미팅이 있어서요.

week 03

나를 위한 Push-up! 자기계발&문화생활

day 11 영어공부

day 12 자기계발

day 13 인맥관리

day 14 진학과 어학연수

day 15 체력단련

day 11 영어공부

자기계발 목록 1순위, 영어 정복!
영어를 배우는 것과 관련된 표현입니다.
음원을 듣고 영어표현을 따라 말한 후, 손으로 써보세요.

1st step ★ 따라 **말**하고 **써**보며 표현 **익**히기

음원 듣기

❶ 외국인과 영어로 의사소통하다 ▸ communicate with foreigners in English

❷ 단어를 암기하다 ▸ memorize English words

❸ 영어 받아쓰기를 하다 ▸ do English dictation

❹ 실수를 하면서 배우다 ▸ learn by making mistakes

❺ 영어학원에 다니다 ▸ go to the English academy

❻ 자신감을 가지고 말하다 ▸ speak with confidence

❼ 영어를 유창하게 말하다 ▸ speak English fluently

❽ 영어가 안 는다 ▸ English is not improving

앞에서 배운 표현을 떠올리며 한글에 해당하는 영어문장을 만들어보세요.

전체 문장을 만드는 게 어렵다면 오른쪽 옆 페이지를 참고하세요.

2nd step ★ 문장 속 표현 **확인**하기

❶ 저도 당신처럼 영어로 외국인과 대화하고 싶어요.

❷ 암기할 영어 단어가 너무 많아요.

❸ 영어 받아쓰기가 당신의 듣기 실력을 길러줄 거예요.

❹ 사람들은 실수를 하면서 언어를 배워요.

❺ 저는 일 끝나고 영어학원에 가요.

❻ 자신감을 가지고 말하세요!

❼ 언젠가는 나도 영어가 유창해지겠지.

❽ 왜 내 영어는 안 느는 걸까?

ANSWER ❶ I would like to communicate with foreigners in English like you. ❷ There are so many English words to memorize. ❸ English dictation will improve your listening skills. ❹ People learn languages by making mistakes. ❺ I go to the English Academy after work. ❻ Speak with confidence! ❼ One day I will speak English fluently. ❽ Why isn't my English improving?

빈칸에 해당하는 표현을 채우며 한 번 더 복습해보세요.

먼저 만든 전체 문장을 떠올리며 빈칸을 채워보세요.

3rd step ★ 한 번 **더 더블**체크!

❶ I would like to ______________ like you.
→ 외국인과 영어로 의사소통하다

❷ There are so many ______________ to ______________ .
→ 영어 단어들, 암기하다

❸ ______________ will improve your listening skills.
→ 영어 받아쓰기를 하는 것

❹ People ______________ languages ______________ .
→ 실수를 하면서 배우다

❺ I ______________ after work.
→ 영어 학원에 다니다

❻ ______________ !
→ 자신감을 가지고 말하다

❼ One day I will ______________ .
→ 영어를 유창하게 말하다

❽ Why isn't my ______________ ?
→ 영어가 안 는다

ANSWER ❶ communicate with foreigners in English ❷ English words, memorize ❸ Doing English dictation ❹ learn, by making mistakes ❺ go to the English academy ❻ speak with confidence ❼ speak English fluently ❽ English improving

음원을 듣고 영어문장을 받아써보세요.

음원을 들으면서 원어민의 목소리를 성대모사하듯
입으로 소리내어 연습해보세요.

4th step ★ 최종점검! 영어문장 **받아써**보기

음원 듣기

❶ HINT communicate

❷ HINT memorize

❸ HINT dictation, skills

❹ HINT mistakes

❺ HINT academy

❻ HINT confidence

❼ HINT fluently

❽ HINT improving

ANSWER ❶ I would like to communicate with foreigners in English like you. ❷ There are so many English words to memorize. ❸ English dictation will improve your listening skills. ❹ People learn languages by making mistakes. ❺ I go to the English academy after work. ❻ Speak with confidence! ❼ One day I will speak English fluently. ❽ Why isn't my English improving?

day 12 자기계발

동기부여, 독서, 좋은 습관 들이기 등 자기계발과 관련된 표현입니다.

음원을 듣고 영어표현을 따라 말한 후, 손으로 써보세요.

1st step ★ 따라 **말**하고 **써**보며 표현 **익**히기

음원 듣기

1. 동기부여하다 ▶ motivate oneself
2. 자기계발서를 읽다 ▶ read self-help books
3. 행동에 옮기다 ▶ take action
4. ~을 하기 위해 많은 노력을 쏟다 ▶ put in a lot of effort to ~
5. 역량을 갈고 닦다 ▶ sharpen one's skills
6. 외국어 능력을 기르다 ▶ build foreign language skills
7. ~하는 습관을 만들다 ▶ make a habit of ~
8. 일과 삶의 균형을 유지하다 ▶ maintain a work-life balance

앞에서 배운 표현을 떠올리며 한글에 해당하는 영어문장을 만들어보세요.

전체 문장을 만드는 게 어렵다면 오른쪽 옆 페이지를 참고하세요.

2nd step ★ 문장 속 표현 **확인**하기

❶ 목표를 이루기 위해 동기부여하는 것은 중요하죠.

❷ 저는 동기부여를 하기 위해 종종 자기계발서를 읽어요.

❸ 목표를 성취하려면 내일이 아닌 지금 행동에 옮기세요.

❹ 저는 외국어 능력을 계발하기 위해 많은 노력을 쏟습니다.

❺ 독서는 네 역량을 갈고 닦는 데 도움을 줄 거야.

❻ 나는 일과 외국어 능력 기르기를 동시에 하느라 바쁜 삶을 살아.

❼ 저는 책 읽는 습관을 만들려고 독서모임에 가입했어요.

❽ 일과 삶의 균형을 유지함으로써, 당신은 좋은 생활방식을 가질 수 있어요.

ANSWER ❶ It's important to motivate yourself in order to achieve your goal. ❷ I often read self-help books to motivate myself. ❸ Take action now to achieve your goal, not tomorrow. ❹ I put in a lot of effort to improve my language skills. ❺ Reading will help you sharpen your skills. ❻ I live a busy life working and building foreign language skills at the same time. ❼ I joined a book club to make a habit of reading. ❽ By maintaining a healthy work-life balance, you can have a good lifestyle.

빈칸에 해당하는 표현을 채우며 한 번 더 복습해보세요.

먼저 만든 전체 문장을 떠올리며 빈칸을 채워보세요.

3rd step ★ 한 번 **더 더블**체크!

❶ It's important to ______ in order to achieve your goal.
→ 동기부여하다

❷ I often ______ to motivate myself.
→ 자기계발서를 읽다

❸ ______ now to achieve your goal, not tomorrow.
→ 행동에 옮기다

❹ I ______ improve my language skills.
→ ~을 하기 위해 많은 노력을 쏟다

❺ Reading will help you ______.
→ 역량을 갈고 닦다

❻ I live a busy life working and ______ at the same time.
→ 외국어 능력을 기르는 것

❼ I joined a book club to ______ reading.
→ ~하는 습관을 만들다

❽ By ______ healthy ______, you can have a good lifestyle.
→ 일과 삶의 균형을 유지하는 것

ANSWER ❶ motivate yourself ❷ read self-help books ❸ Take action ❹ put in a lot of effort to ❺ sharpen your skills ❻ building foreign language skills ❼ make a habit of ❽ maintaining a, work-life balance

음원을 듣고 영어문장을 받아써보세요.

음원을 들으면서 원어민의 목소리를 성대모사하듯
입으로 소리내어 연습해보세요.

음원 듣기

4th step ★ 최종점검! 영어문장 **받아써**보기

❶ HINT order, achieve

❷ HINT motivate

❸ HINT action

❹ HINT effort, improve

❺ HINT sharpen

❻ HINT building

❼ HINT joined, habit

❽ HINT maintaining

ANSWER ❶ It's important to motivate yourself in order to achieve your goal. ❷ I often read self-help books to motivate myself. ❸ Take action now to achieve your goal, not tomorrow. ❹ I put in a lot of effort to improve my language skills. ❺ Reading will help you sharpen your skills. ❻ I live a busy life working and building foreign language skills at the same time. ❼ I joined a book club to make a habit of reading. ❽ By maintaining a healthy work-life balance, you can have a good lifestyle.

day 13 인맥관리

평소 어떤 사람들을 알고 지내는지, SNS, 모임 참여, 연락, 교제 등 인맥관리와 관련된 표현입니다.

음원을 듣고 영어표현을 따라 말한 후, 손으로 써보세요.

1st step ★ 따라 **말**하고 **써**보며 표현 **익**히기

음원 듣기

❶ 인맥을 넓히다 ▸ expand one's network

❷ 편한 자리에 머물다 ▸ stay inside one's comfort zone

❸ 사회 모임에 참여하다 ▸ attend social gatherings

❹ (사람들과) 어울려 교제하다 ▸ socialize (with people)

❺ ~와 연락하고 지내다 ▸ keep in touch with ~

❻ 트렌드를 따라가다/읽다 ▸ keep up with trends

❼ SNS에 정보를 올리다 ▸ post information on social media

❽ 생각을 공유하다 ▸ share ideas

앞에서 배운 표현을 떠올리며 한글에 해당하는 영어문장을 만들어보세요.

전체 문장을 만드는 게 어렵다면 오른쪽 옆 페이지를 참고하세요.

2nd step ★ 문장 속 표현 **확인**하기

❶ 와! 이 행사는 네 인맥을 넓히는 데 도움이 될 거야.

❷ 저는 편한 자리에 있는 것을 선호해요.

❸ 저는 참석하는 사회 모임이 몇 개 있어요.

❹ 저는 사람들과 어울리는 것을 그다지 좋아하지 않지만, 제 남편은 좋아해요.

❺ 페이스북은 지인들이나 옛 친구들과 연락하고 지내는 데 좋아.

❻ 저는 트렌드를 읽고 새로운 사람들을 만나기 위해 정기적으로 IT 학회에 참석해요.

❼ SNS에 정기적으로 좋은 정보를 올려보면 어때?

❽ 나는 새로운 사람들을 만나서 새로운 생각을 공유하는 것을 좋아해.

ANSWER ❶ Come! This event will help you expand your network. ❷ I prefer to stay inside my comfort zone. ❸ I have a few social gatherings that I attend. ❹ I don't like to socialize with people much but my husband does. ❺ Facebook is great for keeping in touch with acquaintances and old friends. ❻ I regularly attend IT conferences to keep up with trends and meet new people. ❼ How about you try posting good information on social media sites on a regular basis? ❽ I like to meet new faces and share new ideas.

빈칸에 해당하는 표현을 채우며 한 번 더 복습해보세요.

먼저 만든 전체 문장을 떠올리며 빈칸을 채워보세요.

3rd step ★ 한 번 **더 더블**체크!

❶ Come! This event will help you ______________ .
→ 인맥을 넓히다

❷ I prefer to ______________ .
→ 편한 자리에 머물다

❸ I have a few ______________ that I ______ .
→ 사회 모임들, 참여하다

❹ I don't like to ______ with people much but my husband does.
→ 어울려 교제하다

❺ Facebook is great for ______________ acquaintances and old friends.
→ ~와 연락하고 지내는 것

❻ I regularly attend IT conferences to ______________ and meet new people.
→ 트렌드를 따라가다

❼ How about you try ______ good ______________ sites on a regular basis?
→ SNS에 정보를 올리는 것

❽ I like to meet new faces and ______ new ______ .
→ 생각을 공유하다

ANSWER ❶ expand your network ❷ stay inside my comfort zone ❸ social gatherings, attend ❹ socialize ❺ keeping in touch with ❻ keep up with trends ❼ posting, information on social media ❽ share, ideas

음원을 듣고 영어문장을 받아써보세요.

음원을 들으면서 원어민의 목소리를 성대모사하듯 입으로 소리내어 연습해보세요.

음원 듣기

4th step ★ 최종점검! 영어문장 **받아써**보기

❶ HINT expand

❷ HINT comfort

❸ HINT gatherings

❹ HINT socialize

❺ HINT acquaintances

❻ HINT regularly, conferences

❼ HINT posting, sites

❽ HINT share

ANSWER ❶ Come! This event will help you expand your network. ❷ I prefer to stay inside my comfort zone. ❸ I have a few social gatherings that I attend. ❹ I don't like to socialize with people much but my husband does. ❺ Facebook is great for keeping in touch with acquaintances and old friends. ❻ I regularly attend IT conferences to keep up with trends and meet new people. ❼ How about you try posting good information on social media sites on a regular basis? ❽ I like to meet new faces and share new ideas.

진학과 해외연수

학위 취득, 진로 변경, 안식년 등
진학과 해외연수에 관련된 표현입니다.

음원을 듣고 영어표현을 따라 말한 후, 손으로 써보세요.

1st step ★ 따라 **말**하고 **써**보며 표현 **익**히기

음원 듣기

1. 석사/박사 학위를 따다 ▶ get a master's/doctoral degree
2. 공부를 계속하다 ▶ pursue one's education
3. (고속) 승진하다, 출세하다 ▶ move up the ranks
4. (직업상) 진로를 바꾸다 ▶ make a career change
5. 새로운 환경으로 나가다, 편한 곳 밖으로 나오다 ▶ step outside one's comfort zone
6. ~에 대한 이해를 깊게 하다 ▶ deepen one's understanding of ~
7. 재정 문제를 해결하다 ▶ deal with financial problems
8. 직장생활을 중단하다, 안식년을 갖다 ▶ take a career break

앞에서 배운 진표현을 떠올리며 한글에 해당하는 영어문장을 만들어보세요.

전체 문장을 만드는 게 어렵다면 오른쪽 옆 페이지를 참고하세요.

2nd step ★ 문장 속 표현 **확인**하기

❶ 석사학위를 따는 것이 꼭 필요할까요?

❷ 저는 일을 그만두고 공부를 하고 싶어요.

❸ 승진하고 싶다면, 석사학위를 따는 게 좋을 거예요.

❹ 진로를 변경해볼 생각이야.

❺ 너만의 세상 밖으로 나와서 새로운 것들을 시도해봐!

❻ 해외연수는 세상에 대한 이해를 깊게 해줄 거예요.

❼ 나는 공부하는 동안 재정 문제들을 해결해야 할 거야.

❽ 게일은 안식년을 갖는 동안 여행을 많이 했어.

ANSWER ❶ Is getting a master's degree necessary? ❷ I would like to quit my job and pursue my education. ❸ You'd better get a master's degree if you want to move up the ranks. ❹ I am thinking of making a career change. ❺ Step outside your comfort zone and try new things! ❻ Studying abroad will deepen your understanding of the world. ❼ I will have to deal with financial problems while studying. ❽ Gayle traveled a lot while taking her career break.

빈칸에 해당하는 표현을 채우며 한 번 더 복습해보세요.

먼저 만든 전체 문장을 떠올리며 빈칸을 채워보세요.

3rd step ★ 한 번 **더 더블**체크!

❶ Is ________________ necessary?
→ 석사 학위를 따는 것

❷ I would like to quit my job and ________________.
→ 공부를 계속하다

❸ You'd better get a master's degree if you want to ________________.
→ (고속) 승진하다

❹ I am thinking of ________________.
→ 진로를 바꾸는 것

❺ ________________ and try new things!
→ 새로운 환경으로 (편한 곳 밖으로) 나가다

❻ Studying abroad will ________________ the world.
→ ~에 대한 이해를 깊게 하다

❼ I will have to ________________ while studying.
→ 재정 문제들을 해결하다

❽ Gayle traveled a lot while ________ her ________.
→ 안식년을 갖는 중에

ANSWER ❶ getting a master's degree ❷ pursue my education ❸ move up the ranks ❹ making a career change ❺ Step outside your comfort zone ❻ deepen your understanding of ❼ deal with financial problems ❽ taking, career break

음원을 듣고 영어문장을 받아써보세요.

음원을 들으면서 원어민의 목소리를 성대모사하듯 입으로 소리내어 연습해보세요.

4th step ★ 최종점검! 영어문장 **받아써**보기 음원 듣기

❶ HINT necessary

❷ HINT pursue

❸ HINT the, ranks

❹ HINT career, change

❺ HINT step, comfort

❻ HINT deepen

❼ HINT financial

❽ HINT while

ANSWER ❶ Is getting a master's degree necessary? ❷ I would like to quit my job and pursue my education. ❸ You'd better get a master's degree if you want to move up the ranks. ❹ I am thinking of making a career change. ❺ Step outside your comfort zone and try new things! ❻ Studying abroad will deepen your understanding of the world. ❼ I will have to deal with financial problems while studying. ❽ Gayle traveled a lot while taking her career break.

day 15 체력단련

근력 운동, 자전거 타기, 다이어트 등
체력단련과 관련된 표현입니다.

음원을 듣고 영어표현을 따라 말한 후, 손으로 써보세요.

1st step ★ 따라 **말**하고 **써**보며 표현 **익**히기

음원 듣기

❶ 체육관에 등록하다 ▶ join the gym

❷ 근력 운동을 하다 ▶ lift weights

❸ 러닝머신에서 뛰다 ▶ run on the treadmill

❹ 운동용 자전거를 타다 ▶ ride the stationary bike

❺ 스트레칭하다 ▶ do stretching

❻ 윗몸 일으키기를 하다 ▶ do sit-ups

❼ 다이어트를 하다 ▶ go on a diet

❽ 체력을 유지하다 ▶ stay in shape

앞에서 배운 표현을 떠올리며 한글에 해당하는 영어문장을 만들어보세요.

전체 문장을 만드는 게 어렵다면 오른쪽 옆 페이지를 참고하세요.

2nd step ★ 문장 속 표현 **확인**하기

❶ 나 올해는 헬스장에 등록할 거야.

❷ 나 근육 만들려고 근력 운동 중이야.

❸ 나는 속도 7로 러닝머신 위에서 뛰어.

❹ 그리고 나서 운동용 자전거를 40분 동안 타.

❺ 컴퓨터 앞에 앉아 있는 동안 스트레칭을 좀 하는 게 어때?

❻ 저는 뱃살을 없애려고 윗몸 일으키기를 해요.

❼ 지난 6개월 동안 살이 좀 쪄서 지금 다이어트 중이야.

❽ 나는 규칙적으로 운동을 해서 체력을 유지할 수 있어.

ANSWER ❶ I am joining the gym this year. ❷ I lift weights to build muscle. ❸ I run on the treadmill at the speed of 7 km/h. ❹ And I ride the stationary bike for 40 minutes. ❺ How about doing some stretching while you are sitting at the computer? ❻ I do sit-ups to lose my belly fat. ❼ I gained some weight for the last 6 months so I am going on a diet now. ❽ I exercise regularly so I can stay in shape.

빈칸에 해당하는 표현을 채우며 한 번 더 복습해보세요.

먼저 만든 전체 문장을 떠올리며 빈칸을 채워보세요.

3rd step ★ 한 번 **더 더블**체크!

❶ I am ______ ______ ______ this year.
→ 체육관에 등록하다

• be -ing는 가까운 미래를 나타냄

❷ I ______ ______ to build muscle.
→ 근력 운동을 하다

❸ I ______ ______ ______ ______ at the speed of 7km/h.
→ 러닝머신에서 뛰다

❹ And I ______ ______ ______ ______ for 40 minutes.
→ 운동용 자전거를 타다

❺ How about ______ some ______ while you are sitting at the computer? → 스트레칭하는 것

❻ I ______ ______ to lose my belly fat.
→ 윗몸 일으키기를 하다

❼ I gained some weight for the last 6 months so I am ______ ______ ______ ______ now.
→ 다이어트 중이다

❽ I exercise regularly so I can ______ ______ ______.
→ 체력을 유지하다

ANSWER ❶ joining the gym ❷ lift weights ❸ run on the treadmill ❹ ride the stationary bike ❺ doing, stretching ❻ do sit-ups ❼ go on a diet ❽ stay in shape

음원을 듣고 영어문장을 받아써보세요.

음원을 들으면서 원어민의 목소리를 성대모사하듯 입으로 소리내어 연습해보세요.

4th step ★ 최종점검! 영어문장 **받아써**보기

음원 듣기

❶ HINT gym

❷ HINT muscle

❸ HINT treadmill

❹ HINT stationary

❺ HINT stretching

❻ HINT sit-ups, belly

❼ HINT gained

❽ HINT regularly, shape

ANSWER ❶ I am joining the gym this year. ❷ I lift weights to build muscle. ❸ I run on the treadmill at the speed of 7 km/h. ❹ And I ride the stationary bike for 40 minutes. ❺ How about doing some stretching while you are sitting at the computer? ❻ I do sit-ups to lose my belly fat. ❼ I gained some weight for the last 6 months so I am going on a diet now. ❽ I exercise regularly so I can stay in shape.

나를 위한 Push-up! 자기계발&문화생활

자기계발과 관련된 표현들로 이루어진 실제 대화에 도전!
음원을 들으며 영어문장을 따라 말해보세요.

음원 듣기

Ⓐ My English is still not improving. I still make a lot of mistakes.

Ⓑ People learn by making mistakes.

Ⓐ How do you speak English so fluently? Have you studied abroad?

Ⓑ I have been recording sentences for the past 3 years. Also, I try to socialize with foreign coworkers.

Ⓐ Unbelievable! How could you do that every day for 3 years?

Ⓑ I read a self-help book. It said that you need to make a habit of something if you want to achieve it. So I did it.

Ⓐ 여전히 영어가 안 늘어. 나는 여전히 실수를 많이 해.

Ⓑ 사람은 실수를 하면서 배워.

Ⓐ 너는 어떻게 그렇게 영어를 유창하게 해? 외국에서 공부했어?

Ⓑ 나는 3년 동안 매일 문장들을 녹음해왔어. 또, 외국인 동료들과 사귀려고 노력해.

Ⓐ 놀랍다! 어떻게 3년 동안이나 매일 그걸 할 수 있었어?

Ⓑ 내가 자기계발서를 하나 읽었는데, 책에서 말하길, 이루고 싶은 게 있다면 습관으로 만들어야 한대. 그래서 그렇게 했지.

week 04

먹고 마시고~ 음식&술

음식과 레스토랑 1

먹고 싶은 음식, 식욕, 맛 표현 등 먹고 마시는 음식과 관련된 표현입니다.

음원을 듣고 영어표현을 따라 말한 후, 손으로 써보세요.

1st step ★ 따라 **말**하고 **써**보며 표현 **익**히기

음원 듣기

❶ ~이 너무 먹고 싶다 ▸ crave

❷ 식욕이 없다, 식욕을 잃다 ▸ lose one's appetite

❸ 입맛을 돋우다 ▸ regain one's appetite

❹ 내 주변 맛집을 찾다 ▸ find the best restaurant near me

❺ 더치페이하다 ▸ go Dutch

❻ 맛이 이상하다 ▸ taste funny/weird

❼ 끝맛이 안 좋다 ▸ have a bad aftertaste

❽ ~에 알레르기가 있다 ▸ be allergic to ~

day 16

앞에서 배운 표현을 떠올리며 한글에 해당하는 영어문장을 만들어보세요.

전체 문장을 만드는 게 어렵다면 오른쪽 옆 페이지를 참고하세요.

2nd step ★ 문장 속 표현 **확인**하기

❶ 초콜릿이 너무 먹고 싶어.

❷ 나 입맛이 없어.

❸ 냉면이 네 입맛을 돋울 수 있을 거야.

❹ 내가 우리 근처에 맛집을 몇 개 찾아놨어.

❺ 우리 매번 그랬던 것처럼 더치페이하자.

❻ 맛이 이상해.

❼ 이 된장찌개는 끝맛이 안 좋아.

❽ 미안하지만 저는 생선을 못 먹어요. 알레르기가 있어요.

ANSWER ❶ I am craving chocolate. ❷ I lost my appetite. ❸ Cold noodles can help you regain your appetite. ❹ I found some of the best restaurants near us. ❺ Let's go Dutch like we always do. ❻ It tastes funny. ❼ This soybean soup has a bad aftertaste. ❽ I am sorry I can't eat fish. I'm allergic to it.

빈칸에 해당하는 표현을 채우며 한 번 더 복습해보세요.

먼저 만든 전체 문장을 떠올리며 빈칸을 채워보세요.

3rd step ★ 한 번 **더 더블**체크!

❶ I am ________ chocolate.
→ ~이 너무 먹고 싶다

❷ I ________ ________ ________ .
→ 식욕을 잃었다
• lose의 과거형은 lost

❸ Cold noodles can help you ________ ________ ________ .
→ 입맛을 돋우다

❹ I ________ some of ________ ________ ________ ________ us.
→ 주변 맛집을 찾았다

❺ Let's ________ ________ like we always do.
→ 더치페이하다

❻ It ________ ________ .
→ 맛이 이상하다
• 3인칭 단수 주어는 동사에 s 붙이기

❼ This soybean soup ________ ________ ________ ________ .
→ 끝맛이 안 좋다

❽ I am sorry I can't eat fish. I'm ________ ________ it.
→ ~에 알레르기가 있다

ANSWER ❶ craving ❷ lost my appetite ❸ regain your appetite ❹ found, the best restaurants near ❺ go Dutch ❻ tastes funny ❼ has a bad aftertaste ❽ allergic to

음원을 듣고 영어문장을 받아써보세요.

음원을 들으면서 원어민의 목소리를 성대모사하듯 입으로 소리내어 연습해보세요.

4th step ★ 최종점검! 영어문장 **받아써**보기 음원 듣기

❶ HINT craving

❷ HINT appetite

❸ HINT regain, appetite

❹ HINT restaurants, near

❺ HINT Dutch

❻ HINT funny

❼ HINT soybean

❽ HINT allergic

ANSWER ❶ I am craving chocolate. ❷ I lost my appetite. ❸ Cold noodles can help you regain your appetite. ❹ I found some of the best restaurants near us. ❺ Let's go Dutch like we always do. ❻ It tastes funny. ❼ This soybean soup has a bad aftertaste. ❽ I am sorry I can't eat fish. I'm allergic to it.

day 17 음식과 레스토랑 2

익은 정도, 간, 디저트, 웨이팅 등
음식과 레스토랑에 관련된 표현입니다.

음원을 듣고 영어표현을 따라 말한 후, 손으로 써보세요.

1st step ★ 따라 **말**하고 **써**보며 표현 **익**히기

음원 듣기

❶ 덜 익다 ▶ be undercooked

❷ 너무 익다 ▶ be overcooked

❸ 간이 덜 되다 ▶ be under-seasoned

❹ 잘 익다 ▶ be well-cooked[well-done]

❺ 음식에 뭔가가 있다 ▶ There be something in this food

❻ 줄 서서 기다리다 ▶ wait in line

❼ 음식을 포장해서 가다 ▶ get food to go

❽ 디저트를 먹을 여유가 있다 ▶ have space for dessert

앞에서 배운 표현을 떠올리며 한글에 해당하는 영어문장을 만들어보세요.

전체 문장을 만드는 게 어렵다면 오른쪽 옆 페이지를 참고하세요.

2nd step ★ 문장 속 표현 **확인**하기

❶ 야채가 덜 익었어.

❷ 고기가 너무 익었어.

❸ 음식이 간이 덜 되었어.

❹ 고기가 잘 익었어.

❺ 이 음식에 뭔가가 있어요.

❻ 그 파스타 집은 기다렸다가 먹을 가치가 있어.

❼ 이거 포장해 갈게요.

❽ 아직 디저트 배는 따로 있지!

ANSWER ❶ The vegetables are undercooked. ❷ The meat is overcooked. ❸ The food is under-seasoned. ❹ The meat is well-cooked[done]. ❺ There is something in this food. ❻ The pasta place is worth waiting in line for. ❼ I would like to get this to go. ❽ I still have space for dessert!

빈칸에 해당하는 표현을 채우며 한 번 더 복습해보세요.

먼저 만든 전체 문장을 떠올리며 빈칸을 채워보세요.

3rd step ★ 한 번 **더 더블**체크!

❶ The vegetables ________ ________ .
→ 덜 익다

❷ The meat ________ ________ .
→ 너무 익다

❸ The food ________ ________ .
→ 간이 덜 되다

❹ The meat ________ ________ .
→ 잘 익다

❺ There is ________ ________ ________ ________ .
→ 음식에 뭔가가 있다

❻ The pasta place is worth ________ ________ ________ for.
→ 줄 서서 기다리는 것

❼ I would like to ________ this ________ ________ .
→ 음식을 포장해서 가다

❽ I still ________ ________ ________ ________ !
→ 디저트를 먹을 여유가 있다

ANSWER ❶ are undercooked ❷ is overcooked ❸ is under-seasoned ❹ is well-cooked[done] ❺ something in this food ❻ waiting in line ❼ get, to go ❽ have space for dessert

음원을 듣고 영어문장을 받아써보세요.

음원을 들으면서 원어민의 목소리를 성대모사하듯 입으로 소리내어 연습해보세요.

음원 듣기

4th step ★ 최종점검! 영어문장 **받아써**보기

❶ HINT vegetables

❷ HINT meat

❸ HINT under-seasoned

❹ HINT well-cooked

❺ HINT something

❻ HINT place, worth

❼ HINT would

❽ HINT space

ANSWER ❶ The vegetables are undercooked. ❷ The meat is overcooked. ❸ The food is under-seasoned. ❹ The meat is well-cooked. ❺ There is something in this food. ❻ The pasta place is worth waiting in line for. ❼ I would like to get this to go. ❽ I still have space for dessert.

day 18 맛

싱겁고, 기름지고, 쫄깃하고, 바삭바삭한 맛과 관련된 표현입니다.

음원을 듣고 영어표현을 따라 말한 후, 손으로 써보세요.

1st step ★ 따라 **말**하고 **써**보며 표현 **익**히기

음원 듣기

❶ 맛있는/맛있다 ▶ (be) tasty

❷ 싱거운/싱겁다 ▶ (be) bland

❸ 질긴, 쫄깃한/쫄깃하다 ▶ (be) chewy

❹ 기름진/기름지다 ▶ (be) greasy

❺ 바삭한/바삭바삭하다 ▶ (be) crispy

❻ (건강한 맛의) 고소한/고소하다 ▶ (be) wholesome

❼ (크림 파스타 등이) 크리미한/크리미하다 ▶ (be) creamy

❽ 맛이 이상한/이상하다 ▶ (be) funny[weird]

앞에서 배운 표현을 떠올리며 한글에 해당하는 영어문장을 만들어보세요.

전체 문장을 만드는 게 어렵다면 오른쪽 옆 페이지를 참고하세요.

2nd step ★ 문장 속 표현 **확인**하기

❶ 맛이 어때? – 엄청 맛있어!

❷ 매운 소스가 없으니, 면이 좀 싱겁네.

❸ 고기가 너무 구워졌나봐. 좀 질겨.

❹ 나 요즘 기름진 음식을 줄이고 있어.

❺ 치킨 껍질 좀 봐! 엄청 바삭바삭해 보여.

❻ 현미밥이 고소하네요.

❼ 저는 여기서 항상 크림이 듬뿍 든 로제 파스타를 시켜요.

❽ 된장찌개에 뭐 넣었어? 맛이 이상해.

ANSWER ❶ How does that taste? – It's so tasty. ❷ Without spicy sauce, the noodles are bland. ❸ I think the meat is overcooked. It is a little chewy. ❹ I am cutting down on greasy food these days. ❺ Look at the chicken skin! Looks so crispy. ❻ Brown rice is wholesome. ❼ I always order creamy rosé pasta here. ❽ What did you put in the soybean soup? It tastes funny.

빈칸에 해당하는 표현을 채우며 한 번 더 복습해보세요.

먼저 만든 전체 문장을 떠올리며 빈칸을 채워보세요.

3rd step ★ 한 번 **더 더블**체크!

❶ How does that taste? – It's so ________ .
→ 맛있다

❷ Without spicy sauce, the noodles ________ ________ .
→ 싱겁다

❸ I think the meat is overcooked. It ________ a little ________ .
→ 질기다

❹ I am cutting down on ________ food these days.
→ 기름진

❺ Look at the chicken skin! Looks so ________ .
→ 바삭바삭한

❻ Brown rice ________ ________ .
→ 고소하다

❼ I always order ________ rosé pasta here.
→ 크리미한

❽ What did you put in the soybean soup? It tastes ________ .
→ 맛이 이상한

ANSWER ❶ tasty ❷ are bland ❸ is, chewy ❹ greasy ❺ crispy ❻ is wholesome ❼ creamy ❽ funny

음원을 듣고 영어문장을 받아써보세요.

음원을 들으면서 원어민의 목소리를 성대모사하듯 입으로 소리내어 연습해보세요.

4th step ★ 최종점검! 영어문장 **받아써**보기 　음원 듣기

❶ HINT tasty

❷ HINT sauce, bland

❸ HINT chewy

❹ HINT greasy

❺ HINT skin

❻ HINT wholesome

❼ HINT rosé, pasta

❽ HINT soybean

ANSWER ❶ How does that taste? – It's so tasty. ❷ Without spicy sauce, the noodles are bland. ❸ I think the meat is overcooked. It is a little chewy. ❹ I am cutting down on greasy food these days. ❺ Look at the chicken skin! Looks so crispy. ❻ Brown rice is wholesome. ❼ I always order creamy rosé pasta here. ❽ What did you put in the soybean soup? It tastes funny.

day 19 술자리 1

주량, 취기, 한잔하기 등
술자리와 관련된 표현입니다.

음원을 듣고 영어표현을 따라 말한 후, 손으로 써보세요.

1st step ★ 따라 **말**하고 **써**보며 표현 **익**히기

음원 듣기

❶ 술 한잔하러 가다 ▸ go for a drink

❷ 2차를 가다 ▸ go for round two

❸ 한 모금만 마시다 ▸ have a sip

❹ 술이 세다 ▸ be a good drinker

❺ 술이 약하다 ▸ be a light weight drinker

❻ 멀쩡하다 ▸ be sober

❼ 취하다 ▸ be drunk

❽ 취기가 있다, 알딸딸하다 ▸ be tipsy

앞에서 배운 표현을 떠올리며 한글에 해당하는 영어문장을 만들어보세요.

전체 문장을 만드는 게 어렵다면 오른쪽 옆 페이지를 참고하세요.

2nd step ★ 문장 속 표현 **확인**하기

❶ 금요일에 시간 돼? 술 한잔하러 가자.

❷ 2차 가자!

❸ 전 이따가 미팅이 있어서 한 모금만 할게요.

❹ 나는 술이 센 편이야.

❺ 소주 한 잔에 토를 했어? 너 술 엄청 약하구나.

❻ 걱정하지 마. 나 멀쩡해.

❼ 그는 완전 취했어.

❽ 나 조금 취기가 올라.

ANSWER ❶ Are you free on Friday? Let's go for a drink. ❷ Let's go for round two. ❸ Sorry I will just have a sip. I have a meeting later. ❹ I am a good drinker. ❺ You threw up after a shot of soju? What a light weight drinker. ❻ Don't worry. I am sober. ❼ He's so drunk. ❽ I am a little tipsy.

빈칸에 해당하는 표현을 채우며 한 번 더 복습해보세요.

먼저 만든 전체 문장을 떠올리며 빈칸을 채워보세요.

3rd step ★ 한 번 **더 더블**체크!

❶ Are you free on Friday? Let's ________ ________ ________ ________ .
→ 술 한잔하러 가다

❷ Let's ________ ________ ________ ________ .
→ 2차를 가다

❸ Sorry I will just ________ ________ ________ . I have a meeting later.
→ 한 모금만 마시다

❹ I ________ ________ ________ ________ .
→ 술이 세다

❺ You threw up after a shot of soju? What ________ ________ ________ ________ .
→ 술이 약한 사람

❻ Don't worry. I ________ ________ .
→ 멀쩡하다

❼ He's so ________ .
→ 취했다

❽ I ________ a little ________ .
→ 취기가 있다

ANSWER ❶ go for a drink ❷ go for round two ❸ have a sip ❹ am a good drinker ❺ a light weight drinker ❻ am sober ❼ drunk ❽ am, tipsy

음원을 듣고 영어문장을 받아써보세요.

음원을 들으면서 원어민의 목소리를 성대모사하듯 입으로 소리내어 연습해보세요.

4th step ★ 최종점검! 영어문장 **받아써**보기

음원 듣기 

❶ HINT free, on

❷ HINT round

❸ HINT sip

❹ HINT good

❺ HINT threw, shot

❻ HINT sober

❼ HINT drunk

❽ HINT tipsy

ANSWER ❶ Are you free on Friday? Let's go for a drink. ❷ Let's go for round two. ❸ Sorry I will just have a sip. I have a meeting later. ❹ I am a good drinker. ❺ You threw up after a shot of soju? What a light weight drinker. ❻ Don't worry. I am sober. ❼ He's so drunk. ❽ I am a little tipsy.

day 20 술자리 2

숙취, 필름 끊김, 혀 꼬임, 절주, 폭음 등
술자리와 관련된 표현입니다.

음원을 듣고 영어표현을 따라 말한 후, 손으로 써보세요.

1st step ★ 따라 **말**하고 **써**보며 표현 **익**히기

음원 듣기

❶ 필름이 끊기다 ▶ black out

❷ 혀가 꼬이다 ▶ slur one's words

❸ 숙취가 있다 ▶ have a hangover

❹ ~에게 술을 사다 ▶ buy+사람+a drink

❺ 사교용 음주를 좋아하다 ▶ like social drinking(= be a social drinker)

❻ 술을 줄이다 ▶ cut down on alcohol/drinking

❼ 술을 잘 절제하다 ▶ drink in moderation

❽ 폭음하다 ▶ binge-drink

앞에서 배운 표현을 떠올리며 한글에 해당하는 영어문장을 만들어보세요.

전체 문장을 만드는 게 어렵다면 오른쪽 옆 페이지를 참고하세요.

2nd step ★ 문장 속 표현 **확인**하기

❶ 나 어제 필름이 끊긴 게 틀림 없어.

❷ 너 말이 다 꼬여.

❸ 나 숙취가 심해. 숙취 없애는 데 뭐가 좋을까?

❹ 이번 주에 술 한 잔 살게요.

❺ 저는 사교용으로만 술을 마셔요. 거의 회식 때만요.

❻ 술을 줄이려고 노력해보는 게 어때?

❼ 저는 술을 잘 절제해서 마셔요.

❽ 폭음 그만 해. 그거 건강에 정말 안 좋아.

ANSWER ❶ I must have blacked out last night. ❷ You're slurring all of your words. ❸ I have a bad hangover. What can help me get over it? ❹ I will buy you a drink later this week. ❺ I am only a social drinker. I drink only at work outings. ❻ How about you try cutting down on alcohol? ❼ I drink in moderation. ❽ Stop binge-drinking. It's really bad for your health.

빈칸에 해당하는 표현을 채우며 한 번 더 복습해보세요.

먼저 만든 전체 문장을 떠올리며 빈칸을 채워보세요.

3rd step ★ 한 번 **더 더블**체크!

❶ I must have ________ ________ last night.
→ 필름이 끊겼다

❷ You're ________ all of ________ ________.
→ 혀가 꼬인다

❸ I ________ ________ bad ________. What can help me get over it?
→ 숙취가 있다

❹ I will ________ you ________ ________ later this week.
→ ~에게 술을 사다

❺ I am only a ________ ________. I drink only at work outings.
→ 사교용 음주를 좋아하는 사람

❻ How about you try ________ ________ ________ ________?
→ 술을 줄이는 것

❼ I ________ ________ ________.
→ 술을 잘 절제하다

❽ Stop ________. It's really bad for your health.
→ 폭음하는 것

ANSWER ❶ blacked out ❷ slurring, your words ❸ have a, hangover ❹ buy, a drink ❺ social drinker ❻ cutting down on alcohol ❼ drink in moderation ❽ binge-drinking

음원을 듣고 영어문장을 받아써보세요.

음원을 들으면서 원어민의 목소리를 성대모사하듯 입으로 소리내어 연습해보세요.

4th step ★ 최종점검! 영어문장 **받아써**보기 음원 듣기

❶ HINT blacked

❷ HINT slurring

❸ HINT hangover

❹ HINT will

❺ HINT social, outings

❻ HINT alcohol

❼ HINT moderation

❽ HINT binge-drinking

ANSWER ❶ I must have blacked out last night. ❷ You're slurring all of your words. ❸ I have a bad hangover. What can help me get over it? ❹ I will buy you a drink later this week. ❺ I am only a social drinker. I drink only at work outings. ❻ How about you try cutting down on alcohol? ❼ I drink in moderation. ❽ Stop binge-drinking. It's really bad for your health.

먹고 마시고~ 음식&술

음식과 술에 관련된 표현들로 이루어진 실제 대화에 도전!
음원을 들으며 영어문장을 따라 말해보세요.

음원 듣기

Ⓐ We ordered egg rolls, kimchi stew and 2 bottles of soju.

Ⓑ Sounds good, but two bottles? Who is going to drink so much?

Ⓐ Me. I am craving alcohol. I have been stressed out from work.

Ⓑ Ok, but you shouldn't binge-drink until you black out.

Ⓐ That's why I only ordered 2 bottles. I don't even get tipsy after 2 bottles. Now I drink in moderation.

Ⓑ Ok, I believe you. By the way, I think the egg rolls are a bit bland. Could you pass me the ketchup?

Ⓐ 우리 계란말이랑 김치찌개 그리고 소주 두 병 시켰어.

Ⓑ 좋네. 그런데 두 병? 누가 그렇게 많이 마실 거야?

Ⓐ 나. 나 지금 술 땡기거든. 회사에서 스트레스 받아서.

Ⓑ 그래. 그런데 너 필름 끊길 때까지 폭음하면 안 된다!

Ⓐ 그래서 딱 두 병만 시켰지. 나는 두 병에는 취기도 없어. 요즘 절제해서 마시는 중이라니까.

Ⓑ 그래, 믿을게. 근데 말이야, 계란말이가 좀 싱거운 것 같아. 케첩 좀 건네줄래?

week 05

열심히 달린 나를 위한 선물, 쇼핑&여행

day 21 쇼핑 1

day 22 쇼핑 2

day 23 공항

day 24 여행

day 25 특별한 날 기념하기

day 21 쇼핑 1

옷 입어보기, 할인받기, 선물포장 등
쇼핑과 관련된 표현입니다.

음원을 듣고 영어표현을 따라 말한 후, 손으로 써보세요.

1st step ★ 따라 **말**하고 **써**보며 표현 **익**히기

음원 듣기

❶ 쇼핑을 하다 ▶ do some shopping

❷ 여러 곳을 둘러보다 ▶ shop around

❸ (한번) 입어보다 ▶ try+옷+on

❹ (옷이) 타이트하다/헐겁다 ▶ be tight/loose

❺ (백화점 등) 세일 중이다 ▶ have a sale

❻ 진열되어 있다 ▶ be on display

❼ 할인해주다, 할인받다 ▶ get a discount off/on

❽ 선물포장을 하다 ▶ get+물건+gift-wrapped

앞에서 배운 표현을 떠올리며 한글에 해당하는 영어문장을 만들어보세요.

전체 문장을 만드는 게 어렵다면 오른쪽 옆 페이지를 참고하세요.

2nd step ★ 문장 속 표현 **확인**하기

❶ 쇼핑 좀 해야겠어. 입을 게 없어.

❷ 나는 시간 있을 때 쇼핑할 거 있나 둘러보는 거 좋아해.

❸ 이것들 피팅룸에서 한번 입어봐도 될까요?

❹ 이 셔츠가 좀 타이트하네요. 더 큰 거 있나요?

❺ 유니클로가 지금 빅 세일 중이래.

❻ 저기 진열되어 있는 가방 봐. 매일 들고다닐 가방으로 괜찮아 보여.

❼ 나 이 치마 50% 할인받아서 샀어.

❽ 이거 선물포장할 수 있나요?

ANSWER ❶ I need to do some shopping. I have nothing to wear. ❷ I love to shop around in my free time. ❸ Can I try these on in the fitting room? ❹ This shirt is a little tight. Do you have a bigger one? ❺ Uniqlo is having a big sale now. ❻ Look at the bag on display. It would make a good everyday bag. ❼ I got a 50% discount on this skirt. ❽ Could I get this gift-wrapped?

빈칸에 해당하는 표현을 채우며 한 번 더 복습해보세요.

먼저 만든 전체 문장을 떠올리며 빈칸을 채워보세요.

3rd step ★ 한 번 **더 더블**체크!

---

❶ I need to ______ ______ ______ . I have nothing to wear.
→ 쇼핑을 하다

❷ I love to ______ ______ in my free time.
→ 여러 곳을 둘러보다

❸ Can I ______ these ______ in the fitting room?
→ (한번) 입어보다

❹ This shirt ______ a little ______ . Do you have a bigger one?
→ (옷이) 타이트하다

❺ Uniqlo is ______ ______ big ______ now.
→ (백화점 등) 세일 중이다

❻ Look at the bag ______ ______ . It would make a good everyday bag.
→ 진열되어 있는

❼ I ______ ______ 50% ______ ______ this skirt.
→ 할인받았다

❽ Could I ______ this ______ ?
→ 선물 포장을 하다

ANSWER ❶ do some shopping ❷ shop around ❸ try, on ❹ is, tight ❺ have a, sale ❻ on display ❼ got a, discount on ❽ get, gift-wrapped

음원을 듣고 영어문장을 받아써보세요.

음원을 들으면서 원어민의 목소리를 성대모사하듯 입으로 소리내어 연습해보세요.

4th step ★ 최종점검! 영어문장 **받아써**보기

음원 듣기 

❶ HINT wear

❷ HINT around

❸ HINT fitting

❹ HINT shirt

❺ HINT big

❻ HINT display

❼ HINT skirt

❽ HINT gift-wrapped

ANSWER ❶ I need to do some shopping. I have nothing to wear. ❷ I love to shop around in my free time. ❸ Can I try these on in the fitting room? ❹ This shirt is a little tight. Do you have a bigger one? ❺ Uniqlo is having a big sale now. ❻ Look at the bag on display. It would make a good everyday bag. ❼ I got a 50% discount on this skirt. ❽ Could I get this gift-wrapped?

day 22 쇼핑 2

환불, 주문 취소, 결재 방법 등 쇼핑과 관련된 표현입니다.

음원을 듣고 영어표현을 따라 말한 후, 손으로 써보세요.

1st step ★ 따라 **말**하고 **써**보며 표현 **익**히기

음원 듣기

1. 환불받다 ▸ get a refund
2. 주문을 취소하다 ▸ cancel the order
3. 배송료를 지불하다 ▸ pay for shipping
4. 현금으로 계산하다 ▸ pay in cash
5. 신용카드로 계산하다 ▸ pay by credit card
6. 일시불로 계산하다 ▸ pay in full
7. 할부로 계산하다 ▸ pay in installments
8. 대량 구입하다 ▸ buy in bulk

앞에서 배운 표현을 떠올리며 한글에 해당하는 영어문장을 만들어보세요.

전체 문장을 만드는 게 어렵다면 오른쪽 옆 페이지를 참고하세요.

2nd step ★ 문장 속 표현 **확인**하기

❶ 이거 환불받을 수 있나요?

❷ 주문한 것을 취소하고 싶어요.

❸ 배송료를 내야 하나요?

❹ 현금으로 계산할게요. 그리고 영수증이 필요해요.

❺ 어떻게 지불하시겠어요? 신용카드로, 아니면 현금으로요?

❻ 그거 일시불로 계산할게요.

❼ 3개월 할부로 계산하고 싶어요.

❽ 코스트코에선, 음식을 대량으로 살 수 있어.

ANSWER ❶ Can I get a refund for this one? ❷ I would like to cancel the order I made. ❸ Do I have to pay for shipping? ❹ I will pay in cash and I will need a receipt. ❺ How will you be paying, by credit card or in cash? ❻ I am paying in full for that. ❼ I would like to pay in 3-month installments. ❽ At Costco, you can buy food in bulk.

빈칸에 해당하는 표현을 채우며 한 번 더 복습해보세요.

먼저 만든 전체 문장을 떠올리며 빈칸을 채워보세요.

3rd step ★ 한 번 **더 더블**체크!

❶ Can I ______ ______ ______ for this one?
→ 환불받다

❷ I would like to ______ ______ ______ I made.
→ 주문을 취소하다

❸ Do I have to ______ ______ ______ ?
→ 배송료를 지불하다

❹ I will ______ ______ ______ and I will need a receipt.
→ 현금으로 계산하다

❺ How will you be ______ , ______ ______ ______ or in cash?
→ 신용카드로 계산하다
• be -ing는 가까운 미래를 나타냄

❻ I am ______ ______ ______ for that.
→ 일시불로 계산하다
• be -ing는 가까운 미래를 나타냄

❼ I would like to ______ ______ 3-month ______ .
→ 할부로 계산하다

❽ At Costco, you can ______ food ______ ______ .
→ 대량 구입하다

ANSWER ❶ get a refund ❷ cancel the order ❸ pay for shipping ❹ pay in cash ❺ paying, by credit card ❻ paying in full ❼ pay in, installments ❽ buy, in bulk

음원을 듣고 영어문장을 받아써보세요.

음원을 들으면서 원어민의 목소리를 성대모사하듯 입으로 소리내어 연습해보세요.

음원 듣기 

❶ HINT refund

❷ HINT cancel

❸ HINT shipping

❹ HINT receipt

❺ HINT credit

❻ HINT full

❼ HINT installments

❽ HINT in, bulk

ANSWER ❶ Can I get a refund for this one? ❷ I would like to cancel the order I made. ❸ Do I have to pay for shipping? ❹ I will pay in cash and I will need a receipt. ❺ How will you be paying, by credit card or in cash? ❻ I am paying in full for that. ❼ I would like to pay in 3-month installments. ❽ At Costco, you can buy food in bulk.

day 23 공항

수화물 부치기, 세관, 이륙/착륙 등 공항과 관련된 표현입니다.

음원을 듣고 영어표현을 따라 말한 후, 손으로 써보세요.

1st step ★ 따라 **말**하고 **써**보며 표현 **익**히기

음원 듣기

❶ 가방을 (화물칸에) 부치다 ▸ check the bags (in)

❷ 7kg을 초과하다 ▸ exceed 7kg

❸ 세관을 통과하다 ▸ get through the customs

❹ 의자를 앞으로 당기다 ▸ pull one's seat forward

❺ (팔걸이에서) 팔을 비켜주다 ▸ move one's arm over

❻ 기내식이 서비스되다 ▸ (in-flight) meal be served

❼ 이륙하다/착륙하다 ▸ take off/land

❽ 연결 항공편을 잡다 ▸ catch one's connecting flight

앞에서 배운 표현을 떠올리며 한글에 해당하는 영어문장을 만들어보세요.

전체 문장을 만드는 게 어렵다면 오른쪽 옆 페이지를 참고하세요.

2nd step ★ 문장 속 표현 **확인**하기

❶ 가방을 체크인 데스크에서 화물로 부치셔야 해요.

❷ 기내용 가방은 7kg을 초과하면 안 됩니다.

❸ 세관을 통과하는 데 15분 정도 걸려요.

❹ 의자를 앞으로 좀 당겨주실 수 있을까요?

❺ (팔걸이에서) 팔을 조금만 움직여주시겠어요?

❻ 다음 식사는 언제 나오나요?

❼ (기내 안내방송) 우리는 5분 후에 이륙할 예정입니다.

❽ 제가 연결 항공편을 타야 하는데요. 어느 쪽으로 가야 하나요?

ANSWER ❶ You should check your bags in at the check-in desk. ❷ Your carry-on bag shouldn't exceed 7kg. ❸ It takes about 15 minutes to get through the customs. ❹ Would you mind pulling your seat forward a little bit? ❺ Would you mind moving your arm over a little bit? ❻ When is the next meal going to be served? ❼ We'll be taking off in just 5 minutes. ❽ I have to catch my connecting flight. Which way do I have to go?

빈칸에 해당하는 표현을 채우며 한 번 더 복습해보세요.

먼저 만든 전체 문장을 떠올리며 빈칸을 채워보세요.

3rd step ★ 한 번 **더 더블**체크!

❶ You should ________ your ________ in at the check-in desk.
→ 가방을 (수화물로) 부치다

❷ Your carry-on bag shouldn't ________ ________.
→ 7kg을 초과하다

❸ It takes about 15 minutes to ________ ________ ________ ________.
→ 세관을 통과하다

❹ Would you mind ________ ________ ________ ________ a little bit?
→ 의자를 앞으로 당기다

• mind -ing ~을 꺼리다

❺ Would you mind ________ ________ ________ ________ a little bit?
→ (팔걸이에서) 팔을 비켜주다

❻ When is the next ________ going to ________ ________?
→ 기내식이 서비스되다

❼ We'll be ________ ________ in just 5 minutes.
→ 이륙하다

❽ I have to ________ ________ ________ ________. Which way do I have to go?
→ 연결 항공편을 잡다

ANSWER ❶ check, bags ❷ exceed 7kg ❸ get through the customs ❹ pulling your seat forward ❺ moving your arm over ❻ meal, be served ❼ taking off ❽ catch my connecting flight

음원을 듣고 영어문장을 받아써보세요.

음원을 들으면서 원어민의 목소리를 성대모사하듯
입으로 소리내어 연습해보세요.

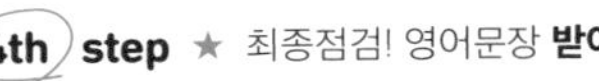

음원 듣기 

❶ HINT check-in

❷ HINT exceed

❸ HINT through, customs

❹ HINT forward

❺ HINT arm, bit

❻ HINT meal, served

❼ HINT minutes

❽ HINT connecting

ANSWER ❶ You should check your bags in at the check-in desk. ❷ Your carry-on bag shouldn't exceed 7kg. ❸ It takes about 15 minutes to get through the customs. ❹ Would you mind pulling your seat forward a little bit? ❺ Would you mind moving your arm over a little bit? ❻ When is the next meal going to be served? ❼ We'll be taking off in just 5 minutes. ❽ I have to catch my connecting flight. Which way do I have to go?

day 24 여행

여행 기간, 짐 싸기, 관광명소 방문 등 여행과 관련된 표현입니다.

음원을 듣고 영어표현을 따라 말한 후, 손으로 써보세요.

1st step ★ 따라 **말**하고 **써**보며 표현 **익**히기

음원 듣기

❶ 당일치기 여행을 가다 ▶ go on a day-trip

❷ 3박 4일로 여행가다 ▶ go on a trip for 4 days and 3 nights

❸ 해외여행을 가다 ▶ go on an overseas trip

❹ 짐을 가볍게/효율적으로 싸다 ▶ pack light/efficiently

❺ 경치를 즐기다 ▶ enjoy the scenery

❻ 역사적인 장소[유적지]를 방문하다 ▶ visit historical sites

❼ 관광명소를 방문하다 ▶ visit tourist attractions

❽ 기념품을 사다 ▶ buy (some) souvenirs

앞에서 배운 표현을 떠올리며 한글에 해당하는 영어문장을 만들어보세요.

전체 문장을 만드는 게 어렵다면 오른쪽 옆 페이지를 참고하세요.

2nd step ★ 문장 속 표현 **확인**하기

❶ 나 평창으로 당일치기 여행 가.

❷ 나 3박 4일로 여행 갈 거야.

❸ 나도 해외여행 가고 싶어.

❹ 나는 여행갈 때 보통 짐을 가볍게 싸.

❺ 여행의 핵심은 현지 경치를 즐기는 것이지.

❻ 역사적인 유적지를 방문함으로써 현지 문화에 대해 많이 배울 수 있어.

❼ 나는 일반 관광객들처럼 관광명소 방문하는 것은 좋아하지 않아.

❽ 기념품 사는 거 돈 낭비라고 생각하지 않아?

ANSWER ❶ I am going on a day-trip to Pyeong-chang. ❷ I am going on a trip for 4 days and 3 nights. ❸ I wish I could go on an overseas trip. ❹ I usually pack light when I go on a trip. ❺ The point of traveling is to enjoy the local scenery. ❻ You can learn about the local culture by visiting historical sites. ❼ I don't like to visit tourist attractions like the typical tourist. ❽ Don't you think buying souvenirs is a waste of money?

빈칸에 해당하는 표현을 채우며 한 번 더 복습해보세요.

먼저 만든 전체 문장을 떠올리며 빈칸을 채워보세요.

3rd step ★ 한 번 **더 더블**체크!

❶ I am ________ to Pyeong-chang.
→ 당일치기 여행을 가다 • be -ing는 가까운 미래를 나타냄

❷ I am ________ 4 days and 3 nights.
→ 3박 4일로 여행가다 • be -ing는 가까운 미래를 나타냄

❸ I wish I could ________ .
→ 해외여행을 가다

❹ I usually ________ when I go on a trip.
→ 짐을 가볍게 싸다

❺ The point of traveling is to ________ local ________ .
→ 경치를 즐기다

❻ You can learn about the local culture by ________ .
→ 역사적인 장소를 방문하다 • by -ing ~함으로써

❼ I don't like to ________ like the typical tourist.
→ 관광명소를 방문하다

❽ Don't you think ________ is a waste of money?
→ 기념품을 사는 것

ANSWER ❶ going on a day-trip ❷ going on a trip for ❸ go on an overseas trip ❹ pack light ❺ enjoy the, scenery ❻ visiting historical sites ❼ visit tourist attractions ❽ buying souvenirs

음원을 듣고 영어문장을 받아써보세요.

음원을 들으면서 원어민의 목소리를 성대모사하듯
입으로 소리내어 연습해보세요.

4th step ★ 최종점검! 영어문장 **받아써**보기

음원 듣기 

❶ HINT day-trip

❷ HINT trip

❸ HINT overseas

❹ HINT pack

❺ HINT local, scenery

❻ HINT historical, sites

❼ HINT attractions, typical

❽ HINT souvenirs, waste

ANSWER ❶ I am going on a day-trip to Pyeong-chang. ❷ I am going on a trip for 4 days and 3 nights. ❸ I wish I could go on an overseas trip. ❹ I usually pack light when I go on a trip. ❺ The point of traveling is to enjoy the local scenery. ❻ You can learn about the local culture by visiting historical sites. ❼ I don't like to visit tourist attractions like the typical tourist. ❽ Don't you think buying souvenirs is a waste of money?

day 25 특별한 날 기념하기

명절, 결혼기념일, 크리스마스, 동창회 등 특별한 날과 관련된 표현입니다.

음원을 듣고 영어표현을 따라 말한 후, 손으로 써보세요.

1st step ★ 따라 **말**하고 **써**보며 표현 **익**히기

음원 듣기

❶ (구정) 설을 쇠다/기념하다 ▶ celebrate the Lunar New Year's Day

❷ 결혼기념일을 기념하다 ▶ celebrate the wedding anniversary

❸ (칠순) 생일파티를 열다 ▶ throw one's (70th) birthday party

❹ 송별파티를 열다 ▶ throw a farewell party

❺ 동창회에서 ▶ at a reunion party

❻ 송년회에서 ▶ at a year-end party

❼ 크리스마스 이브에 ▶ on Christmas Eve

❽ 특별한 때에 ▶ on a special occasion

앞에서 배운 표현을 떠올리며 한글에 해당하는 영어문장을 만들어보세요.

전체 문장을 만드는 게 어렵다면 오른쪽 옆 페이지를 참고하세요.

2nd step ★ 문장 속 표현 **확인**하기

❶ 우리는 음력 달력에 따라 구정 설을 쉽니다.

❷ 어떻게 우리 결혼 30주년을 기념할 수 있을까?

❸ 우리는 뷔페를 빌려서 어머니 칠순잔치를 열 거예요.

❹ 사라를 위해 송별파티를 열어주는 거 어때?

❺ 동창회에서 진숙이를 만났어. 할 말이 얼마나 많았다고.

❻ 게일과 저는 송년회에서 결국 화해했어요.

❼ 너희들 크리스마스이브에 뭐 특별한 거 했어?

❽ 우리는 특별한 날에 이 와인을 딸 거예요.

ANSWER ❶ We celebrate the Lunar New Year according to the Lunar calendar. ❷ How should we celebrate our 30th wedding anniversary? ❸ We are going to have a buffet catered and throw our mother's 70th birthday party. ❹ How about we throw a farewell party for Sera? ❺ I met Jinsook at the reunion party. We had a lot to catch up on. ❻ Gayle and I finally made up at the company's year-end party. ❼ Did you guys do anything special on Christmas Eve? ❽ We are going to open this wine on a special occasion.

빈칸에 해당하는 표현을 채우며 한 번 더 복습해보세요.

먼저 만든 전체 문장을 떠올리며 빈칸을 채워보세요.

3rd step ★ 한 번 **더 더블**체크!

❶ We ______________ according to the Lunar calendar.
→ 구정 설을 쇠다

❷ How should we ______ our 30th ______________?
→ 결혼기념일을 기념하다

❸ We are going to have a buffet catered and ______ our mother's ______________.
→ 칠순 생일파티를 열다

❹ How about we ______________ for Sera?
→ 송별파티를 열다

❺ I met Jinsook ______ the ______________. We had a lot to catch up on.
→ 동창회에서

❻ Gayle and I finally made up ______ the company's ______________.
→ 송년회에서

❼ Did you guys do anything special ______________?
→ 크리스마스 이브에

❽ We are going to open this wine ______________.
→ 특별한 때에

ANSWER ❶ celebrate the Lunar New Year ❷ celebrate, wedding anniversary ❸ throw, 70th birthday party ❹ throw a farewell party ❺ at, reunion party ❻ at, year-end party ❼ on Christmas Eve ❽ on a special occasion

음원을 듣고 영어문장을 받아써보세요.

음원을 들으면서 원어민의 목소리를 성대모사하듯 입으로 소리내어 연습해보세요.

4th step ★ 최종점검! 영어문장 **받아써**보기 음원 듣기

❶ HINT Lunar, according

❷ HINT anniversary

❸ HINT buffet, catered

❹ HINT throw, farewell

❺ HINT reunion, catch

❻ HINT year-end

❼ HINT guys, Eve

❽ HINT wine, occasion

ANSWER ❶ We celebrate the Lunar New Year according to the Lunar calendar. ❷ How should we celebrate our 30th wedding anniversary? ❸ We are going to have a buffet catered and throw our mother's 70th birthday party. ❹ How about we throw a farewell party for Sera? ❺ I met Jinsook at the reunion party. We had a lot to catch up on. ❻ Gayle and I finally made up at the company's year-end party. ❼ Did you guys do anything special on Christmas Eve? ❽ We are going to open this wine on a special occasion.

나를 위한 선물, 쇼핑&여행

쇼핑과 여행에 관련된 표현들로 이루어진 실제 대화에 도전!

음원을 들으며 영어문장을 따라 말해보세요.

음원 듣기

Ⓐ Wow. What are you doing here? You're doing some shopping, aren't you?

Ⓑ Yeah, we are going on a trip for our first wedding anniversary for 2 days. So I was shopping around for it.

Ⓐ Really? They are having a big sale, that's why I'm here right now.

Ⓑ I see. Did you buy that bag here? It looks so cute!

Ⓐ Is it? Thank you. I bought this bag for summer. I paid for it in 3-month installments.

Ⓐ 와, 여기서 뭐해? 쇼핑하는구나, 그렇지?

Ⓑ 응, 우리 2박으로 결혼 1주년 기념 여행가거든. 그래서 둘러보고 있었어.

Ⓐ 정말? 나도 여기 지금 세일 중이어서 온 거야.

Ⓑ 그랬구나. 그 가방 여기서 산 거야? 정말 귀엽다!

Ⓐ 그래? 고마워. 이 가방 여름용으로 샀어. 이거 3개월 할부로 샀어.

week 06

내가 왕년에~~
지난 시절 이야기

day 26 대학시절 1

학점, 전공, 장학금 등
대학시절과 관련된 표현입니다.
음원을 듣고 영어표현을 따라 말한 후, 손으로 써보세요.

1st step ★ 따라 **말**하고 **써**보며 표현 **익**히기

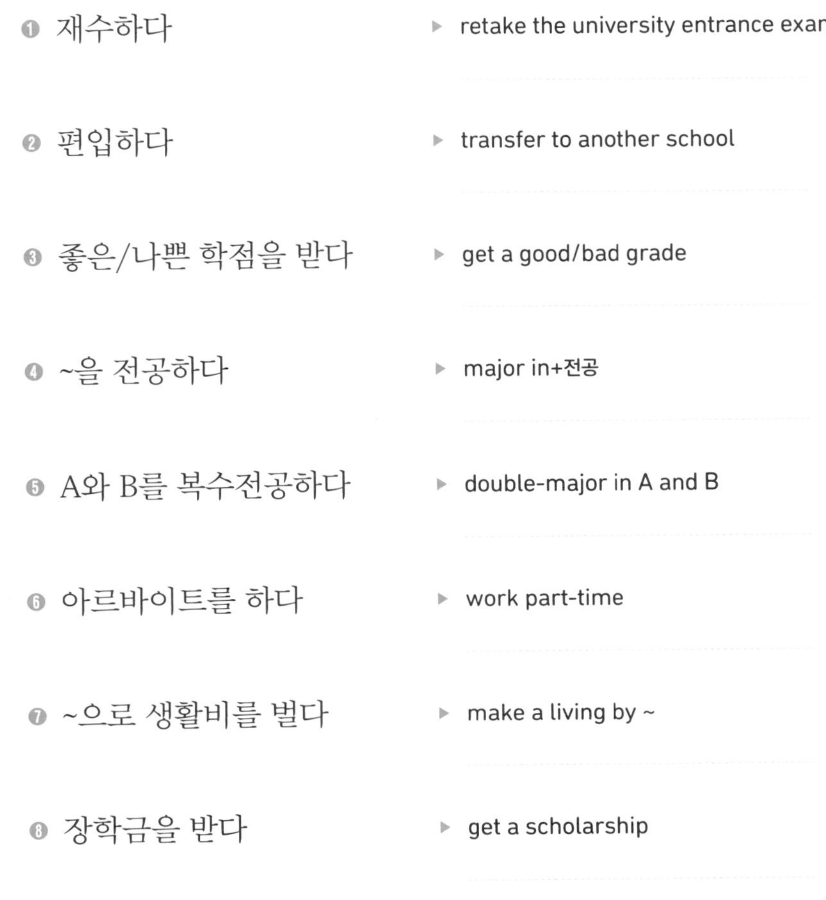

1. 재수하다 ▶ retake the university entrance exam
2. 편입하다 ▶ transfer to another school
3. 좋은/나쁜 학점을 받다 ▶ get a good/bad grade
4. ~을 전공하다 ▶ major in+전공
5. A와 B를 복수전공하다 ▶ double-major in A and B
6. 아르바이트를 하다 ▶ work part-time
7. ~으로 생활비를 벌다 ▶ make a living by ~
8. 장학금을 받다 ▶ get a scholarship

음원 듣기

앞에서 배운 표현을 떠올리며 한글에 해당하는 영어문장을 만들어보세요.

전체 문장을 만드는 게 어렵다면 오른쪽 옆 페이지를 참고하세요.

2nd step ★ 문장 속 표현 **확인**하기

❶ 저는 재수를 해야 했어요.

❷ 저는 고려대학교로 편입했어요.

❸ 이번 학기에 진짜 안 좋은 학점을 받았어요.

❹ 게일은 물리학을 전공해요.

❺ 저는 언론학과 교육학을 복수전공했어요.

❻ 너 요즘 아르바이트해?

❼ 저는 과외로 생활비를 벌었어요.

❽ 저 장학금 받았어요.

ANSWER ❶ I had to retake the university entrance exam. ❷ I transferred to Korea University. ❸ I got really bad grades this semester. ❹ Gayle is majoring in Physics. ❺ I double-majored in Journalism and Education. ❻ Are you working part-time these days? ❼ I made a living by tutoring. ❽ I got a scholarship.

빈칸에 해당하는 표현을 채우며 한 번 더 복습해보세요.

먼저 만든 전체 문장을 떠올리며 빈칸을 채워보세요.

3rd step ★ 한 번 **더 더블**체크!

❶ I had to ________ ________ ________ ________ ________ .
→ 재수하다

❷ I ________ ________ Korea University.
→ 편입했다

❸ I ________ really ________ ________ this semester.
→ 나쁜 학점을 받았다

❹ Gayle is ________ ________ Physics.
→ ~을 전공 중이다

❺ I ________ ________ Journalism ________ Education.
→ 복수전공했다

❻ Are you ________ ________ these days?
→ 아르바이트를 하고 있다

❼ I ________ ________ ________ ________ tutoring.
→ ~으로 생활비를 벌었다

❽ I ________ ________ ________ .
→ 장학금을 받았다

ANSWER ❶ retake the university entrance exam ❷ transferred to ❸ got, bad grades ❹ majoring in ❺ double-majored in, and ❻ working part-time ❼ made a living by ❽ got a scholarship

음원을 듣고 영어문장을 받아써보세요.

음원을 들으면서 원어민의 목소리를 성대모사하듯 입으로 소리내어 연습해보세요.

음원 듣기

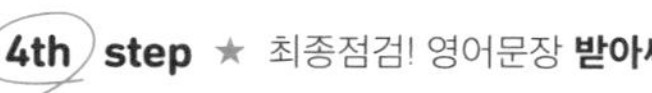

❶ HINT retake, entrance

❷ HINT transferred

❸ HINT semester

❹ HINT Physics

❺ HINT Journalism

❻ HINT these, days

❼ HINT tutoring

❽ HINT scholarship

ANSWER ❶ I had to retake the university entrance exam. ❷ I transferred to Korea University. ❸ I got really bad grades this semester. ❹ Gayle is majoring in Physics. ❺ I double-majored in Journalism and Education. ❻ Are you working part-time these days? ❼ I made a living by tutoring. ❽ I got a scholarship.

day 27 대학시절 2

휴학, 복학, 대학원 진학 등 대학시절과 관련된 표현입니다.

음원을 듣고 영어표현을 따라 말한 후, 손으로 써보세요.

1st step ★ 따라 **말**하고 **써**보며 표현 **익**히기

음원 듣기

❶ 한 학기 휴학하다 ▶ take a semester off

❷ 1년 휴학하다 ▶ take a year off

❸ 회사에서 인턴을 하다 ▶ do an internship at+회사

❹ 복학하다 ▶ go back to school

❺ 컴퓨터 자격증을 따다 ▶ get a computer certification

❻ 어학연수를 하다 ▶ study language abroad

❼ 대학원에 진학하다 ▶ go to graduate school

❽ 취업하다 ▶ get a job

앞에서 배운 표현을 떠올리며 한글에 해당하는 영어문장을 만들어보세요.

전체 문장을 만드는 게 어렵다면 오른쪽 옆 페이지를 참고하세요.

2nd step ★ 문장 속 표현 **확인**하기

❶ 저는 작년에 한 학기를 휴학했어요.

❷ 나는 세계여행하느라 1년 휴학했어.

❸ 저는 지금 한 IT 회사에서 인턴을 하고 있습니다.

❹ 올해 복학할 거예요.

❺ 컴퓨터 자격증을 하나 딸 필요가 있어요.

❻ 영어 어학연수를 갈 생각이에요.

❼ 대학원에 진학할 계획이에요.

❽ 게일은 졸업 전에 취업했어. 운이 좋았지.

ANSWER ❶ I took a semester off last year. ❷ I took a year off to travel around the world. ❸ I am doing an internship at an IT firm. ❹ I will go back to school this year. ❺ I should get a computer certification. ❻ I am thinking about studying English abroad. ❼ I am planning to go to graduate school. ❽ Gayle got a job before graduation. She was lucky.

빈칸에 해당하는 표현을 채우며 한 번 더 복습해보세요.

먼저 만든 전체 문장을 떠올리며 빈칸을 채워보세요.

3rd step ★ 한 번 **더 더블**체크!

❶ I ________________ last year
→ 한 학기 휴학했다

❷ I ________________ to travel around the world.
→ 1년 휴학했다

❸ I am ________________ an IT firm.
→ ~에서 인턴을 하고 있다

❹ And I will ________________ this year.
→ 복학하다

❺ I should ________________.
→ 컴퓨터 자격증을 따다

❻ I am thinking about ________ English ________.
→ 어학연수를 하는 것

❼ I am planning to ________________.
→ 대학원에 진학하다

❽ Gayle ________________ before graduation. She was lucky.
→ 취업했다

ANSWER ❶ took a semester off ❷ took a year off ❸ doing an internship at ❹ go back to school ❺ get a computer certification ❻ studying, abroad ❼ go to graduate school ❽ got a job

음원을 듣고 영어문장을 받아써보세요.

음원을 들으면서 원어민의 목소리를 성대모사하듯 입으로 소리내어 연습해보세요.

 ★ 최종점검! 영어문장 **받아써**보기

음원 듣기 

❶ HINT semester

❷ HINT around

❸ HINT IT, firm

❹ HINT will

❺ HINT certification

❻ HINT abroad

❼ HINT planning

❽ HINT graduation

ANSWER ❶ I took a semester off last year. ❷ I took a year off to travel around the world. ❸ I am doing an internship at an IT firm. ❹ I will go back to school this year. ❺ I should get a computer certification. ❻ I am thinking about studying English abroad. ❼ I am planning to go to graduate school. ❽ Gayle got a job before graduation. She was lucky.

day 28 중고등학교 시절

문과/이과, 모의고사, 입시 등 중고등학교 시절과 관련된 표현입니다.

음원을 듣고 영어표현을 따라 말한 후, 손으로 써보세요.

1st step ★ 따라 **말**하고 **써**보며 표현 **익**히기

음원 듣기

❶ 중간/기말고사가 있다 ▸ have a mid-term/final (exam)

❷ 모의고사를 보다 ▸ take a mock test

❸ 시험을 잘 보다 ▸ do well on an exam

❹ 입시(보습) 학원에 가다 ▸ go to a cram school

❺ 찍기를 잘하다 ▸ be good at guessing

❻ 중퇴하다 ▸ drop out of school

❼ 검정고시를 보다 ▸ take Korean GED(General Equivalency Diploma)

❽ 문과, 이과, 예체능 ▸ humanities, natural sciences, art & music & PE(Physical Education)

앞에서 배운 표현을 떠올리며 한글에 해당하는 영어문장을 만들어보세요.

전체 문장을 만드는 게 어렵다면 오른쪽 옆 페이지를 참고하세요.

2nd step ★ 문장 속 표현 **확인**하기

❶ 다음 주 월요일에 중간고사가 있어요.

❷ 수능 전에 두어 번의 모의고사를 봐야 해요.

❸ 나는 시험 잘 봤었어.

❹ 나는 입시학원에 가느라 많은 시간을 보냈어.

❺ 나는 객관식에서 찍기를 잘해.

❻ 그는 중학교 2학년 마치고 중퇴했어.

❼ 저는 검정고시를 봤어요.

❽ 고등학교에는 3개의 전공이 있는데, 문과, 이과 그리고 예체능이다.

ANSWER ❶ I have a mid-term exam next Monday. ❷ I have to take a couple of mock tests before the actual Korean SAT. ❸ I used to do well on exams. ❹ I spent a lot of time going to cram schools. ❺ I am good at guessing on multiple-choice questions. ❻ He dropped out of school after his second year of middle school. ❼ I took the Korean GED. ❽ There are 3 streams of study in high school; humanities, natural sciences and art&music&PE.

빈칸에 해당하는 표현을 채우며 한 번 더 복습해보세요.

먼저 만든 전체 문장을 떠올리며 빈칸을 채워보세요.

3rd step ★ 한 번 **더 더블**체크!

❶ I ____ ____ ____ ____ next Monday.
→ 중간고사가 있다

❷ I have to ____ ____ couple of ____ ____ before the actual Korean SAT. → 모의고사를 보다

❸ I used to ____ ____ ____ exams.
→ 시험을 잘 보다

❹ I spent a lot of time ____ ____ ____ schools.
→ 입시학원에 가다 • spend -ing ~하는 데 시간을 보내다

❺ I ____ ____ ____ ____ on multiple-choice questions.
→ 찍기를 잘하다

❻ He ____ ____ ____ ____ after his second year of middle school. → 중퇴했다

❼ I ____ the ____ ____ .
→ 검정고시를 봤다

❽ There are 3 streams of study in high school;
____ , ____ ____ and ____ .
→ 문과, 이과, 예체능

ANSWER ❶ have a mid-term exam ❷ take a, mock tests ❸ do well on ❹ go to cram ❺ am good at guessing ❻ dropped out of school ❼ took, Korean GED ❽ humanities, natural sciences, art&music&PE

음원을 듣고 영어문장을 받아써보세요.

음원을 들으면서 원어민의 목소리를 성대모사하듯 입으로 소리내어 연습해보세요.

4th step ★ 최종점검! 영어문장 **받아써**보기

음원 듣기 

❶ HINT mid-term

❷ HINT mock, actual

❸ HINT well

❹ HINT cram

❺ HINT multiple-choice

❻ HINT second

❼ HINT GED

❽ HINT streams, humanities

ANSWER ❶ I have a mid-term exam next Monday. ❷ I have to take a couple of mock tests before the actual Korean SAT. ❸ I used to do well on exams. ❹ I spent a lot of time going to cram schools. ❺ I am good at guessing on multiple-choice questions. ❻ He dropped out of school after his second year of middle school. ❼ I took the Korean GED. ❽ There are 3 streams of study in high school; humanities, natural sciences and art&music&PE.

day 29 군대 시절

훈련소, 휴가, 군복무 등
군대 시절과 관련된 표현입니다.

음원을 듣고 영어표현을 따라 말한 후, 손으로 써보세요.

1st step ★ 따라 **말**하고 **써**보며 표현 **익**히기

음원 듣기

❶ 군복무를 하다 ▶ do one's military service

❷ 훈련소로 가다 ▶ go to boot camp

❸ 공익 요원으로 복무하다 ▶ work as a civil servant

❹ 현역에서 제외되다 ▶ be exempted from active service

❺ 휴가 나오다 ▶ get leave

❻ 군복무를 마치다 ▶ finish the military

❼ 예비군으로 있다 ▶ be in the army reserve

❽ 민방위에 소속되다 ▶ be in the civil defense unit

앞에서 배운 표현을 떠올리며 한글에 해당하는 영어문장을 만들어보세요.

전체 문장을 만드는 게 어렵다면 오른쪽 옆 페이지를 참고하세요.

2nd step ★ 문장 속 표현 **확인**하기

❶ 저는 2014년부터 2016년까지 군복무를 했어요.

❷ 우리가 제일 처음 하는 일은 훈련소에 가는 겁니다.

❸ 저는 공익근무 요원으로 복무했어요.

❹ 그는 어떤 이유론지 현역에서 제외되었다.

❺ 나는 휴가 나오면 많은 친구들을 만났다.

❻ 저는 전역하자마자, 복학했어요.

❼ 너는 아직 예비군이구나.

❽ 나는 민방위 2년차야.

ANSWER ❶ I did my military service from 2014 to 2016. ❷ The first thing we do is go to boot camp. ❸ I worked as a civil servant. ❹ He was exempted from active service for some reason. ❺ Whenever I got leave, I met a lot of friends. ❻ As soon as I finished my military, I went back to school. ❼ You are still in the army reserve. ❽ I have been in the civil defense unit for 2 years.

빈칸에 해당하는 표현을 채우며 한 번 더 복습해보세요.

먼저 만든 전체 문장을 떠올리며 빈칸을 채워보세요.

❶ I ______ ______ ______ ______ from 2014 to 2016.
→ 군복무했다

❷ The first thing we do is ______ ______ ______ ______ .
→ 훈련소로 가다

❸ I ______ ______ ______ ______ ______ .
→ 공익 요원으로 복무했다

❹ He ______ ______ ______ ______ ______ for some reason.
→ 현역에서 제외되었다

❺ Whenever I ______ ______ , I met a lot of friends.
→ 휴가를 나왔다

• leave 휴가

❻ As soon as I ______ my ______ , I went back to school.
→ 군복무를 마쳤다

❼ You ______ still ______ ______ ______ ______ .
→ 예비군으로 있다

❽ I have ______ ______ ______ ______ ______ for 2 years.
→ 민방위에 소속되어 있다

ANSWER ❶ did my military service ❷ go to boot camp ❸ worked as a civil servant ❹ was exempted from active service ❺ got leave ❻ finished, military ❼ are, in the army reserve ❽ been in the civil defense unit

음원을 듣고 영어문장을 받아써보세요.

음원을 들으면서 원어민의 목소리를 성대모사하듯 입으로 소리내어 연습해보세요.

4th step ★ 최종점검! 영어문장 **받아써**보기

음원 듣기 

❶ HINT military

❷ HINT boot, camp

❸ HINT civil, servant

❹ HINT exempted

❺ HINT met

❻ HINT military

❼ HINT army, reserve

❽ HINT defense, unit

ANSWER ❶ I did my military service from 2014 to 2016. ❷ The first thing we do is go to boot camp. ❸ I worked as a civil servant. ❹ He was exempted from active service for some reason. ❺ Whenever I got leave, I met a lot of friends. ❻ As soon as I finished my military, I went back to school. ❼ You are still in the army reserve. ❽ I have been in the civil defense unit for 2 years.

day 30 특정일 회상

어린 시절, 학창시절, 전성기 시절 등
과거의 특정 시기와 관련된 표현입니다.

음원을 듣고 영어표현을 따라 말한 후, 손으로 써보세요.

1st step ★ 따라 **말**하고 **써**보며 표현 **익**히기

음원 듣기

❶ (학교 가기 전) 어린 시절에 ▸ in my childhood

❷ 학창시절에 ▸ (back) in my school days

❸ 옛날에는 ▸ (back) in the day

❹ 80년대에는 ▸ in the 80s

❺ 전성기 때 ▸ at the height of one's career

❻ 재작년에 (지 지난주에) ▸ the year before last (the week before last)

❼ 지 지난주 금요일 ▸ the Friday before last

❽ 지난 몇 년 동안 ▸ for the last few years

앞에서 배운 표현을 떠올리며 한글에 해당하는 영어문장을 만들어보세요.

전체 문장을 만드는 게 어렵다면 오른쪽 옆 페이지를 참고하세요.

2nd step ★ 문장 속 표현 **확인**하기

❶ 어렸을 때, 나는 부모님 말을 잘 듣지 않았어.

❷ HOT는 내 학창시절에 정말 인기가 많았어.

❸ 옛날에 우리는 비디오 테이프에 TV 쇼를 녹화하곤 했어.

❹ 나는 이 카페 인테리어가 좋아. 80년대에 와 있는 것 같아.

❺ 그녀는 왜 전성기에 일을 그만두려고 하는 거야?

❻ 진숙이는 재작년에 결혼했어요.

❼ 나 지 지난주 금요일에 집에 있었어.

❽ 사업 때문에 지난 몇 년 간 중국에 살았어요.

ANSWER ❶ In my childhood, I didn't listen to my parents much. ❷ HOT was really popular in my school days. ❸ We used to record TV shows on a videotape back in the day. ❹ I like this cafe interior. I feel like I am in the 80s. ❺ Why is she quitting her job at the height of her career? ❻ Jinsook got married the year before last. ❼ I was at home the Friday before last. ❽ I have lived in China for the last few years because of my business.

빈칸에 해당하는 표현을 채우며 한 번 더 복습해보세요.

먼저 만든 전체 문장을 떠올리며 빈칸을 채워보세요.

3rd step ★ 한 번 **더 더블**체크!

❶ ________________, I didn't listen to my parents much.
→ 어린 시절에

❷ HOT was really popular ________________.
→ 학창시절에

❸ We used to record TV shows on a videotape back ________________.
→ 옛날에

❹ I like this cafe interior. I feel like I am ________________.
→ 80년대에

❺ Why is she quitting her job ________________?
→ ~의 전성기 때

❻ Jinsook got married ________________.
→ 재작년에

❼ I was at home ________________.
→ 지 지난주 금요일

❽ I have lived in China ________________ because of my business.
→ 지난 몇 년 동안

ANSWER ❶ In my childhood ❷ in my school days ❸ in the day ❹ in the 80s ❺ at the height of her career ❻ the year before last ❼ the Friday before last ❽ for the last few years

음원을 듣고 영어문장을 받아써보세요.

음원을 들으면서 원어민의 목소리를 성대모사하듯 입으로 소리내어 연습해보세요.

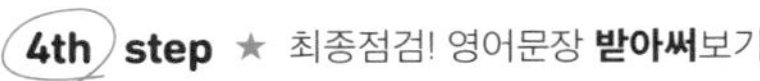

음원 듣기 

❶ HINT childhood

❷ HINT popular

❸ HINT record, videotape

❹ HINT interior

❺ HINT quitting, career

❻ HINT married

❼ HINT at, home

❽ HINT few

ANSWER ❶ In my childhood, I didn't listen to my parents much. ❷ HOT was really popular in my school days. ❸ We used to record TV shows on a videotape back in the day? ❹ I like this cafe interior. I feel like I am in the 80s. ❺ Why is she quitting her job at the height of her career? ❻ Jinsook got married the year before last. ❼ I was at home the Friday before last. ❽ I have lived in China for the last few years because of my business.

내가 왕년에~~ 지난 시절 이야기

과거의 특정 시절과 관련된 표현들로 이루어진 실제 대화에 도전!
음원을 들으며 영어문장을 따라 말해보세요.

음원 듣기

Ⓐ My friend Nari dropped out of high school and now she became a famous singer-song writer.

Ⓑ Awesome. Back in my school days, all I did was go to school, cram schools and do homework.

Ⓐ I think she was so brave at such a young age.

Ⓑ People grow up at different stages. To me, I grew up a lot when I took a year off and worked in Australia.

Ⓐ You are right. By the way, where have you been in Australia? I am going to graduate school there.

Ⓑ Oh, are you? I've been to Melbourne. And you?

Ⓐ 제 친구 나리는 고등학교를 중퇴하고 지금은 유명한 싱어송라이터가 되었어요.

Ⓑ 멋지네요. 학교 다닐 때를 돌아보면, 제가 한 거라고는 학교 가고, 입시학원 가고, 숙제한 게 다인데요.

Ⓐ 그렇게 어린 나이에 그녀는 정말 용감했던 것 같아요.

Ⓑ 사람들은 각자 다른 시기에 성장하잖아요. 저는 1년 휴학하고 호주에서 일했을 때 가장 많이 철들었어요.

Ⓐ 맞아요. 그런데, 호주 어디에 있었어요? 저 거기로 대학원 진학할 거거든요.

Ⓑ 오, 그래요? 저는 멜버른에 있었어요. 당신은요?

week 07

사람에 대해 설명하기, 습관&성격&외모

day 31 습관과 버릇 1

다리 흔들기, 손톱 깨물기, 앉는 자세 등
습관과 버릇에 관련된 표현입니다.

음원을 듣고 영어표현을 따라 말한 후, 손으로 써보세요.

1st step ★ 따라 **말**하고 **써**보며 표현 **익**히기

음원 듣기

❶ ~하는 습관/버릇이 있다 ▸ have a habit of ~

❷ 습관을 고치다 ▸ break (up) the habit

❸ 컴퓨터 앞에 구부정히 앉다 ▸ slouch at the computer

❹ 손톱을 깨물다 ▸ bite one's fingernails

❺ 다리를 흔들다 ▸ shake one's leg

❻ 불평이 많다 ▸ complain about things

❼ 모든 일에 "예스"라고 하다 ▸ say "Yes" to everything

❽ 친절하려고 매우 노력하다 ▸ try so hard to be nice

앞에서 배운 표현을 떠올리며 한글에 해당하는 영어문장을 만들어보세요.

전체 문장을 만드는 게 어렵다면 오른쪽 옆 페이지를 참고하세요.

2nd step ★ 문장 속 표현 **확인**하기

❶ 나는 빨대를 씹는 버릇이 있어.

❷ 나는 그 나쁜 습관을 고칠 필요가 있어.

❸ 컴퓨터 앞에 구부정하게 앉는 건 네 허리에 안 좋아.

❹ 나는 손톱을 깨무는 나쁜 버릇이 있어.

❺ 다리 좀 흔들지 말아줄래?

❻ 우리 언니는 항상 불평이 많아.

❼ 모든 일에 "예스"라고 말할 필요는 없어.

❽ 친절하려고 그렇게 힘들게 노력할 필요는 없어.

ANSWER ❶ I have a habit of chewing on straws. ❷ I need to break that bad habit. ❸ Slouching at the computer is bad for your back. ❹ I have a bad habit of biting my fingernails. ❺ Stop shaking your leg, please? ❻ My sister is always complaining about things. ❼ You don't need to say "Yes" to everything. ❽ You don't need to try so hard to be nice.

빈칸에 해당하는 표현을 채우며 한 번 더 복습해보세요.

먼저 만든 전체 문장을 떠올리며 빈칸을 채워보세요.

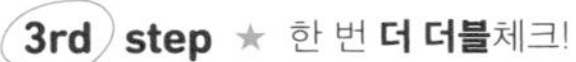

3rd step ★ 한 번 **더 더블**체크!

❶ I ______________ chewing on straws.
→ ~하는 버릇이 있다

❷ I need to ______ that bad ______.
→ 습관을 고치다

❸ ______________ is bad for your back.
→ 컴퓨터 앞에 구부정히 앉는 것

❹ I have a bad habit of ______________.
→ 손톱을 깨무는 것

❺ Stop ______________, please?
→ 다리를 흔드는 것

❻ My sister is always ______________.
→ 불평이 많다

❼ You don't need to ______________.
→ 모든 일에 "예스"라고 하다

❽ You don't need to ______________.
→ 친절하려고 매우 노력하다

ANSWER ❶ have a habit of ❷ break, habit ❸ Slouching at the computer ❹ biting my fingernails ❺ shaking your leg ❻ complain about things ❼ say "Yes" to everything ❽ try so hard to be nice

음원을 듣고 영어문장을 받아써보세요.

음원을 들으면서 원어민의 목소리를 성대모사하듯 입으로 소리내어 연습해보세요.

4th step ★ 최종점검! 영어문장 **받아써**보기

음원 듣기 

❶ HINT chewing, straws

❷ HINT break

❸ HINT slouching

❹ HINT fingernails

❺ HINT shaking

❻ HINT complaining

❼ HINT need

❽ HINT hard

ANSWER ❶ I have a habit of chewing on straws. ❷ I need to break that bad habit. ❸ Slouching at the computer is bad for your back. ❹ I have a bad habit of biting my fingernails. ❺ Stop shaking your leg, please? ❻ My sister is always complaining about things. ❼ You don't need to say "Yes" to everything. ❽ You don't need to try so hard to be nice.

day 32

습관과 버릇 2

식습관, 잠버릇, 구매 습관 등
습관과 버릇에 관련된 표현입니다.

음원을 듣고 영어표현을 따라 말한 후, 손으로 써보세요.

1st step ★ 따라 **말**하고 **써**보며 표현 **익**히기

음원 듣기

❶ 충동구매를 하다 ▶ buy impulsively

❷ 과소비하다 ▶ overspend

❸ 신용카드를 과사용하다 ▶ overuse credit cards

❹ 과식하다 ▶ overeat

❺ 단것을 많이 먹다 ▶ eat too many sweets

❻ 술을 많이 마시다 ▶ drink so much

❼ 늦게 자다 ▶ stay up late

❽ 침대에 누워서 전화를 사용하다 ▶ use one's phone in bed

앞에서 배운 표현을 떠올리며 한글에 해당하는 영어문장을 만들어보세요.

전체 문장을 만드는 게 어렵다면 오른쪽 옆 페이지를 참고하세요.

2nd step ★ 문장 속 표현 **확인**하기

❶ 나는 충동구매를 하는 경향이 있어.

❷ 너 과소비한다고 생각하지 않아?

❸ 신용카드 과사용은 돈 문제를 야기할 거야.

❹ 과식 후에는 체한 것 같은 기분이 들어.

❺ 너 단것을 먹는 게 네 몸에 어떻게 작용하는지 아니?

❻ 너 술을 왜 그렇게 많이 마셔?

❼ 밤 늦게 자는 것은 (너에게) 좋지 않아.

❽ 너 침대에서 전화를 사용하지 않는 게 좋겠어.

ANSWER ❶ I tend to buy impulsively. ❷ Don't you think you are overspending? ❸ Overusing credit cards will cause money problems. ❹ After overeating, I feel like I have an upset stomach. ❺ Do you know what eating sweets does to your body? ❻ Why are you drinking so much? ❼ Staying up late is bad for you. ❽ You shouldn't use your phone in bed.

빈칸에 해당하는 표현을 채우며 한 번 더 복습해보세요.

먼저 만든 전체 문장을 떠올리며 빈칸을 채워보세요.

3rd step ★ 한 번 **더 더블**체크!

❶ I tend to ______________ .
→ 충동구매를 하다

❷ Don't you think you are ______ ?
→ 과소비하고 있다

❸ ______________ will cause money problems.
→ 신용카드를 과사용하는 것

❹ After ______ , I feel like I have an upset stomach.
→ 과식

❺ Do you know what ______________ does to your body?
→ 단것을 먹는 것

❻ Why are you ______________ ?
→ 술을 아주 많이 마시고 있다

❼ ______________ is bad for you.
→ 늦게 자는 것

❽ You shouldn't ______________ .
→ 침대에서 전화를 사용하다

ANSWER ❶ buy impulsively ❷ overspending ❸ Overusing credit cards ❹ overeating ❺ eating sweets ❻ drinking so much ❼ Staying up late ❽ use your phone in bed

음원을 듣고 영어문장을 받아써보세요.

음원을 들으면서 원어민의 목소리를 성대모사하듯 입으로 소리내어 연습해보세요.

4th step ★ 최종점검! 영어문장 **받아써**보기

음원 듣기 

❶ HINT impulsively

❷ HINT overspending

❸ HINT credit, cause

❹ HINT stomach

❺ HINT body

❻ HINT drinking

❼ HINT staying

❽ HINT shouldn't

ANSWER ❶ I tend to buy impulsively. ❷ Don't you think you are overspending? ❸ Overusing credit cards will cause money problems. ❹ After overeating, I feel like I have an upset stomach. ❺ Do you know what eating sweets does to your body? ❻ Why are you drinking so much? ❼ Staying up late is bad for you. ❽ You shouldn't use your phone in bed.

day 33 성격과 성향 1

사교적이고, 느긋하고, 마음씨가 따뜻한 등
성격과 성향에 관련된 표현입니다.

음원을 듣고 영어표현을 따라 말한 후, 손으로 써보세요.

1st step ★ 따라 **말**하고 **써**보며 표현 **익**히기

음원 듣기

❶ 열린 생각을 가지다 ▸ be open-minded

❷ 속이 좁다 ▸ be narrow-minded

❸ 서비스 마인드가 있다 ▸ be service-minded

❹ 마음이 따뜻하다 ▸ be warm-hearted

❺ 마음이 냉정하다 ▸ be cold-hearted

❻ 융통성이 있다(없다) ▸ be (not) flexible

❼ 사교적이다 ▸ be outgoing

❽ 느긋하다 ▸ be easygoing

앞에서 배운 표현을 떠올리며 한글에 해당하는 영어문장을 만들어보세요.

전체 문장을 만드는 게 어렵다면 오른쪽 옆 페이지를 참고하세요.

2nd step ★ 문장 속 표현 **확인**하기

❶ 팀은 오픈 마인드라, 사람을 일방적으로 판단하지 않아.

❷ 너 지금 나한테 속 좁다 그런 거야? 내가 어떻게 그런대?

❸ 승무원은 그녀에게 잘 맞는 직업이야. 그녀는 서비스 마인드가 있어.

❹ 나라는 마음이 따뜻해서 그녀 주변에 사람들이 많아.

❺ 그는 가난한 사람들에 대해 동정심이 없는 걸 보일 때 보면 냉정해 보여.

❻ 내 생각엔 융통성 있는 보스는 없어.

❼ 나는 너의 사교적인 성격을 좋아해.

❽ 내 남편은 느긋한 성격인데 나는 그게 좋더라고.

ANSWER ❶ Tim is open-minded, so he is not judgmental. ❷ Are you saying I am narrow-minded? How so? ❸ A flight attendant is the right job for her. She is service-minded. ❹ Nara is warm-hearted, so there are a lot of people around her. ❺ He looks cold-hearted when he shows no sympathy for poor people. ❻ No boss is flexible in my opinion. ❼ I like your outgoing personality. ❽ My husband is easygoing, and I like that about him.

빈칸에 해당하는 표현을 채우며 한 번 더 복습해보세요.

먼저 만든 전체 문장을 떠올리며 빈칸을 채워보세요.

3rd step ★ 한 번 **더 더블**체크!

❶ Tim ________ ________, so he is not judgmental.
→ 열린 생각을 가지다

❷ Are you saying I ________ ________? How so?
→ 속이 좁다

❸ A flight attendant is the right job for her. She ________ ________.
→ 서비스 마인드가 있다

❹ Nara ________ ________, so there are a lot of people around her.
→ 마음이 따뜻하다

❺ He looks ________ when he shows no sympathy for poor people.
→ 마음이 냉정하다

❻ No boss ________ ________ in my opinion.
→ 융통성이 있다

❼ I like your ________ personality.
→ 사교적이다

❽ My husband ________ ________, and I like that about him.
→ 느긋하다

• easy ① 쉬운, ② 편한

ANSWER ❶ is open-minded ❷ am narrow-minded ❸ is service-minded ❹ is warm-hearted ❺ cold-hearted ❻ is flexible ❼ outgoing ❽ is easygoing

음원을 듣고 영어문장을 받아써보세요.

음원을 들으면서 원어민의 목소리를 성대모사하듯 입으로 소리내어 연습해보세요.

4th step ★ 최종점검! 영어문장 **받아써**보기

음원 듣기

❶ HINT judgmental

❷ HINT narrow-minded

❸ HINT attendant

❹ HINT warm-hearted

❺ HINT sympathy

❻ HINT flexible

❼ HINT personality

❽ HINT easygoing

ANSWER ❶ Tim is open-minded, so he is not judgmental. ❷ Are you saying I am narrow-minded? How so? ❸ A flight attendant is the right job for her. She is service-minded. ❹ Nara is warm-hearted, so there are a lot of people around her. ❺ He looks cold-hearted when he shows no sympathy for poor people. ❻ No boss is flexible in my opinion. ❼ I like your outgoing personality. ❽ My husband is easygoing, and I like that about him.

day 34 성격과 성향 2

가정적이고, 책임감 있고, 유머 감각이 있는 등 성격과 성향에 관련된 표현입니다.

음원을 듣고 영어표현을 따라 말한 후, 손으로 써보세요.

1st step ★ 따라 **말**하고 **써**보며 표현 **익**히기

음원 듣기

❶ 가정적이다 ▸ be family-oriented

❷ 목표 지향적이다 ▸ be goal-oriented

❸ 유머 감각이 있다 ▸ have a sense of humor

❹ 책임감이 있다 ▸ have a sense of responsibility

❺ 자신감이 있다 ▸ be self-confident

❻ 욱하다 ▸ be hot-tempered

❼ 말을 잘하는 사람이다 ▸ be a smooth talker

❽ '예스맨'이다, 복종형이다 ▸ be a yes-person

앞에서 배운 표현을 떠올리며 한글에 해당하는 영어문장을 만들어보세요.

전체 문장을 만드는 게 어렵다면 오른쪽 옆 페이지를 참고하세요.

2nd step ★ 문장 속 표현 **확인**하기

❶ 나는 내 미래의 남편이 가정적이면 좋겠어.

❷ 나는 목표 지향적인 것 같지 않아.

❸ 인간관계에 있어서 유머 감각을 갖는 것은 중요해.

❹ 직장에서 책임감을 가지는 것은 중요하죠.

❺ 나는 모든 일에 자신감을 가지려고 해.

❻ 하워드는 욱하는 성격이 있었는데 지금은 달라.

❼ 그녀는 말을 잘하는 사람이야.

❽ 그는 예스맨이야.

ANSWER ❶ I hope my future husband is family-oriented. ❷ I don't think I am goal-oriented. ❸ Having a sense of humor is important in a relationship. ❹ Having a sense of responsibility is important at work. ❺ I try to be self-confident in everything I do. ❻ Howard used to be hot-tempered, but now he is different. ❼ She's a smooth talker. ❽ He is a yes-man.

빈칸에 해당하는 표현을 채우며 한 번 더 복습해보세요.

먼저 만든 전체 문장을 떠올리며 빈칸을 채워보세요.

3rd step ★ 한 번 **더 더블**체크!

❶ I hope my future husband ________ ________ .
→ 가정적이다

❷ I don't think I ________ ________ .
→ 목표 지향적이다

❸ ________ ________ ________ ________ ________ is important in a relationship.
→ 유머 감각이 있는 것

❹ ________ ________ ________ ________ ________ is important at work.
→ 책임감이 있는 것

❺ I try to ________ ________ in everything I do.
→ 자신감이 있다

❻ Howard used to ________ ________ , but now he is different.
→ 욱하다

❼ She's ________ ________ ________ .
→ 말을 잘하는 사람이다

❽ He ________ ________ ________ .
→ '예스맨'이다

ANSWER ❶ is family-oriented ❷ am goal-oriented ❸ Having a sense of humor ❹ Having a sense of responsibility ❺ be self-confident ❻ be hot-tempered ❼ a smooth talker ❽ be a yes-person

음원을 듣고 영어문장을 받아써보세요.

음원을 들으면서 원어민의 목소리를 성대모사하듯 입으로 소리내어 연습해보세요.

★ 최종점검! 영어문장 **받아써**보기

음원 듣기 

❶ HINT family-oriented

❷ HINT goal-oriented

❸ HINT relationship

❹ HINT responsibility

❺ HINT self-confident

❻ HINT hot-tempered

❼ HINT smooth, talker

❽ HINT yes-man

ANSWER ❶ I hope my future husband is family-oriented. ❷ I don't think I am goal-oriented. ❸ Having a sense of humor is important in a relationship. ❹ Having a sense of responsibility is important at work. ❺ I try to be self-confident in everything I do. ❻ Howard used to be hot-tempered, but now he is different. ❼ She's a smooth talker. ❽ He is a yes-man.

day 35 겉모습 묘사

키, 체형, 얼굴 생김새 등
겉모습 묘사에 관련된 표현입니다.

음원을 듣고 영어표현을 따라 말한 후, 손으로 써보세요.

1st step ★ 따라 **말**하고 **써**보며 표현 **익**히기

음원 듣기

❶ 키가 크다/작다 ▶ be tall/short

❷ 날씬하다 ▶ be slim/thin

❸ 무게가 덜 나가다 ▶ be underweight

❹ 무게가 더 나가다 ▶ be overweight

❺ 평균 체격이다 ▶ be of average build

❻ 평균 키다 ▶ be of average-height

❼ 평균 외모다 ▶ be average-looking

❽ 잘생기다, 예쁘다 ▶ be good-looking

앞에서 배운 표현을 떠올리며 한글에 해당하는 영어문장을 만들어보세요.

전체 문장을 만드는 게 어렵다면 오른쪽 옆 페이지를 참고하세요.

2nd step ★ 문장 속 표현 **확인**하기

❶ 아버지는 키가 큰데 나는 아니야.

❷ 너는 날씬해서 그 드레스가 잘 어울려.

❸ 과체중이나 저체중인 것은 건강에 좋지 않을 수 있어.

❹ 그는 여전히 몸무게가 좀 나가.

❺ 게일은 평균 체격이야.

❻ 한국 여자들의 평균 키가 몇이야?

❼ 평균 외모의 사람들이 오래 보면 더 매력 있어.

❽ 박 씨는 그렇게 잘생기지는 않은 것 같아.

ANSWER ❶ My father is tall, but I am not. ❷ You are slim and look good in that dress. ❸ Being overweight or underweight can be bad for your health. ❹ He is still a bit overweight. ❺ Gayle is of average build. ❻ What is the average height of Korean women? ❼ Average-looking people look more attractive the longer you look at them. ❽ I don't think Mr. Park is that good-looking.

빈칸에 해당하는 표현을 채우며 한 번 더 복습해보세요.

먼저 만든 전체 문장을 떠올리며 빈칸을 채워보세요.

3rd step ★ 한 번 **더 더블**체크!

❶ My father ________ ________ , but I am not.
→ 키가 크다

❷ You ________ ________ and look good in that dress.
→ 날씬하다

❸ ________ overweight or ________ can be bad for your health.
→ 무게가 덜 나가는 것

❹ He ________ still a bit ________ .
→ 무게가 더 나가다

❺ Gayle ________ ________ ________ ________ .
→ 평균 체격이다

• build 명사로 쓰면 '체격'

❻ What ________ the ________ ________ of Korean women?
→ 평균 키다

• height 키[haɪt]: [헤잇]처럼 보이나 [하잇]처럼 발음됨

❼ ________ people look more attractive the longer you look at them.
→ 평균 외모다

❽ I don't think Mr. Park ________ that ________ .
→ 잘생기다, 예쁘다

ANSWER ❶ is tall ❷ are slim ❸ Being, underweight ❹ is, overweight ❺ is of average build ❻ is, average height ❼ Average-looking ❽ is, good-looking

음원을 듣고 영어문장을 받아써보세요.

음원을 들으면서 원어민의 목소리를 성대모사하듯 입으로 소리내어 연습해보세요.

4th step ★ 최종점검! 영어문장 **받아써**보기 음원 듣기

❶ HINT tall

❷ HINT slim

❸ HINT underweight

❹ HINT overweight

❺ HINT average

❻ HINT height

❼ HINT attractive

❽ HINT good-looking

ANSWER ❶ My father is tall, but I am not. ❷ You are slim and look good in that dress. ❸ Being overweight or underweight can be bad for your health. ❹ He is still a bit overweight. ❺ Gayle is of average build. ❻ What is the average height of Korean women? ❼ Average-looking people look more attractive the longer you look at them. ❽ I don't think Mr. Park is that good-looking.

사람에 대한 설명, 습관&성격&외모

습관과 성격, 외모에 관련된 표현들로 이루어진 실제 대화에 도전!
음원을 들으며 영어문장을 따라 말해보세요.

음원 듣기

A I heard you are seeing someone. How is it?

B So far so good. I find him really family-oriented and open-minded.

A Oh. He sounds like a good guy. I have a feeling.

B I thought he was trying to be nice at first, but now I know he is truly warm-hearted.

A So romantic! Do you have a photo of him? I am so curious!

B Have a look. He is average-looking but he gets more attractive the longer I look at him.

A 요즘 만나시는 분 있다면서요. 어때요?

B 지금까지는 좋아요. 만나다보니 가정적인 것 같고, 오픈 마인드에요.

A 오. 좋은 남자처럼 들리는데요. 제가 감이 있어요.

B 처음엔 그가 친절하려고 노력하는 것 같았는데, 지금은 정말 따뜻한 사람인 걸 알겠어요.

A 로맨틱하네요! 그분 사진 있어요? 너무 궁금해요!

B 보세요. 그냥 평균 외모에요. 그런데 보면 볼수록 매력 있는 것 같아요.

week 08

관리가 필요한 것들…
건강 관리&돈 관리&자동차 관리

day 36 건강과 병원 1

기침 나고, 체하고, 어디가 아픈…
건강과 병원에 관련된 표현입니다.
음원을 듣고 영어표현을 따라 말한 후, 손으로 써보세요.

1st step ★ 따라 **말**하고 **써**보며 표현 **익**히기

음원 듣기

❶ 어지럽다 ▸ feel dizzy

❷ 체하다 ▸ have an upset stomach

❸ 기침이 나다 ▸ have a cough

❹ 목이 쉬다 ▸ have a scratchy throat

❺ 목이 뻐근하다 ▸ have a stiff neck

❻ ~에 통증이 있다 ▸ have a pain in ~

❼ ~의 증상이 있다 ▸ have symptoms of ~

❽ 약을 복용하다 ▸ take medicine(s)

앞에서 배운 표현을 떠올리며 한글에 해당하는 영어문장을 만들어보세요.

전체 문장을 만드는 게 어렵다면 오른쪽 옆 페이지를 참고하세요.

2nd step ★ 문장 속 표현 **확인**하기

❶ 컴퓨터 앞에 오래 앉아 있으면 어지러움을 느껴요.

❷ 나 체했어. 약 좀 있어?

❸ 감기는 지나갔는데 기침은 아직 남아 있어요.

❹ 아침에는 항상 목이 쉬어요.

❺ 너 목이 뻣뻣하구나. 나 뻐근함 없애는 마사지 부위를 알아.

❻ 무릎에 통증이 있어요.

❼ 나 감기 증상이 있는 것 같아.

❽ 어떤 약을 복용 중이야?

ANSWER ❶ I feel dizzy when looking at the computer too long. ❷ I have an upset stomach. Do you have any medicine? ❸ I just got over a cold but I still have a cough. ❹ I always have a scratchy throat in the morning. ❺ You have a stiff neck. I know just where to massage to make it better. ❻ I have a pain in my knee. ❼ I think I have symptoms of a cold. ❽ What medicines are you taking?

빈칸에 해당하는 표현을 채우며 한 번 더 복습해보세요.

먼저 만든 전체 문장을 떠올리며 빈칸을 채워보세요.

3rd step ★ 한 번 **더 더블**체크!

❶ I ________ ________ when looking at the computer too long.
→ 어지럽다

❷ I ________ ________ ________ ________. Do you have any medicine?
→ 체하다

❸ I just got over ________ ________ but I still have a cough.
→ 기침이 나다

❹ I always ________ ________ ________ ________ in the morning.
→ 목이 쉬다

❺ You ________ ________ ________ ________. I know just where to massage to make it better.
→ 목이 뻐근하다

❻ I ________ ________ ________ ________ my knee.
→ ~에 통증이 있다

❼ I think I ________ ________ ________ a cold.
→ ~의 증상이 있다

❽ What ________ are you ________?
→ 약을 복용 중이다

ANSWER ❶ feel dizzy ❷ have an upset stomach ❸ a cough ❹ have a scratchy throat ❺ have a stiff neck ❻ have a pain in ❼ have symptoms of ❽ medicines, taking

음원을 듣고 영어문장을 받아써보세요.

음원을 들으면서 원어민의 목소리를 성대모사하듯 입으로 소리내어 연습해보세요.

음원 듣기

4th step ★ 최종점검! 영어문장 **받아써**보기

❶ HINT dizzy

❷ HINT stomach

❸ HINT cough

❹ HINT scratchy, throat

❺ HINT stiff, massage

❻ HINT pain, knee

❼ HINT symptoms

❽ HINT medicines

ANSWER ❶ I feel dizzy when looking at the computer too long. ❷ I have an upset stomach. Do you have any medicine? ❸ I just got over a cold but I still have a cough. ❹ I always have a scratchy throat in the morning. ❺ You have a stiff neck. I know just where to massage to make it better. ❻ I have a pain in my knee. ❼ I think I have symptoms of a cold. ❽ What medicines are you taking?

day 37 건강과 병원 2

입원하고, 수술하고, 건강 검진을 받는 등 건강과 병원에 관련된 표현입니다.

음원을 듣고 영어표현을 따라 말한 후, 손으로 써보세요.

1st step ★ 따라 **말**하고 **써**보며 표현 **익**히기

음원 듣기

1. 얼굴이 붓다 ▸ have a puffy face
2. 시력이 나쁘다/좋다 ▸ have bad/good eyes (vision)
3. 치아를 교정하다 ▸ have one's teeth straightened
4. ~를 삐다 ▸ sprain/dislocate+부위
5. ~에 깁스를 하다 ▸ have a cast on one's ~
6. 입원하다 ▸ be hospitalized
7. 수술하다 ▸ have an operation
8. 건강 검진을 받다 ▸ get a medical checkup

앞에서 배운 표현을 떠올리며 한글에 해당하는 영어문장을 만들어보세요.

전체 문장을 만드는 게 어렵다면 오른쪽 옆 페이지를 참고하세요.

2nd step ★ 문장 속 표현 **확인**하기

❶ 어젯밤에 먹은 라면 때문에 얼굴이 부었어.

❷ 저 시력이 안 좋아요. 근시에요.

❸ 나 치아 교정 중이야.

❹ 테니스 치다가 어깨를 삐었어.

❺ 나 발에 깁스 중이라 집에서 못 나가.

❻ 할머니께서 입원 중이셔.

❼ 친구가 저녁에 수술이 잡혀 있어요.

❽ 나 이번 달에 정기 검진 받아야 해.

ANSWER ❶ I have a puffy face from the ramyeon last night. ❷ I have bad eyes. I am nearsighted. ❸ I am having my teeth straightened. ❹ I dislocated my shoulder while playing tennis. ❺ I have a cast on my foot so I can't leave home. ❻ My grandma has been hospitalized. ❼ My friend is having an operation this evening. ❽ I have to get a regular medical checkup this month.

빈칸에 해당하는 표현을 채우며 한 번 더 복습해보세요.

먼저 만든 전체 문장을 떠올리며 빈칸을 채워보세요.

3rd step ★ 한 번 **더 더블**체크!

❶ I ________________ from the ramyeon last night.
→ 얼굴이 붓다

❷ I ________________. I am nearsighted.
→ 시력이 나쁘다

❸ I am ________________.
→ 치아를 교정 중이다

❹ I ________ my shoulder while playing tennis.
→ ~를 삐었다

❺ I ________________ foot so I can't leave home.
→ ~에 깁스를 하다

❻ My grandma has ________________.
→ 입원 중이다

❼ My friend is ________________ this evening.
→ 수술 예정이다

❽ I have to ________ regular ________ this month.
→ 건강 검진을 받다

ANSWER ❶ have a puffy face ❷ have bad eyes ❸ having my teeth straightened ❹ dislocated ❺ have a cast on my ❻ been hospitalized ❼ having an operation ❽ get a, medical checkup

음원을 듣고 영어문장을 받아써보세요.

음원을 들으면서 원어민의 목소리를 성대모사하듯 입으로 소리내어 연습해보세요.

step ★ 최종점검! 영어문장 **받아써**보기 음원 듣기

❶ HINT puffy, ramyeon

❷ HINT nearsighted

❸ HINT straightened

❹ HINT dislocated

❺ HINT cast

❻ HINT hospitalized

❼ HINT operation

❽ HINT regular

ANSWER ❶ I have a puffy face from the ramyeon last night. ❷ I have bad eyes. I am nearsighted. ❸ I am having my teeth straightened. ❹ I dislocated my shoulder while playing tennis. ❺ I have a cast on my foot so I can't leave home. ❻ My grandma has been hospitalized. ❼ My friend is having an operation this evening. ❽ I have to get a regular medical checkup this month.

day 38 돈 관리&재테크 1

적금, 노후 대비, 소비 줄이기 등
돈 관리와 재테크에 관련된 표현입니다.
음원을 듣고 영어표현을 따라 말한 후, 손으로 써보세요.

1st step ★ 따라 **말**하고 **써**보며 표현 **익**히기

음원 듣기

❶ 돈을 마련해두다 ▸ set money aside

❷ 소비를 줄이다 ▸ cut back on spending

❸ 소비내역을 추적하다 ▸ track one's spending

❹ 여기저기서 사다 ▸ buy here and there

❺ 적금을 들다 ▸ put money into a savings account

❻ 충동구매하다 ▸ do impulse buying

❼ ~을 할부로 사다 ▸ buy+물건+in installments

❽ 카드 빚을 갚다 ▸ pay on credit card debt

day 38

앞에서 배운 표현을 떠올리며 한글에 해당하는 영어문장을 만들어보세요.

전체 문장을 만드는 게 어렵다면 오른쪽 옆 페이지를 참고하세요.

2nd step ★ 문장 속 표현 **확인**하기

❶ 너 은퇴에 대비해 돈 관리를 해야지.

❷ 나는 소비를 줄인다면 이 생활 방식을 유지할 수 없을 거야.

❸ 나는 소비내역을 추적해서 어디에 과소비했는지를 알게 됐어.

❹ 여기저기서 조금씩 산 게 전부인데, 내 돈은 다 어디 갔지?

❺ 나는 돈을 적금 계좌에 넣어.

❻ 나도 내가 충동구매를 그만둬야 한다는 거 알아.

❼ 36개월 할부로 차 한 대 뽑았어.

❽ 나는 매달 카드 빚을 갚느라 고생해.

ANSWER ❶ You should set money aside for retirement. ❷ I wouldn't be able to maintain my current lifestyle if I cut back on spending. ❸ I found out where I overspent by tracking my spending. ❹ I just bought a few things here and there but where did all of my money go? ❺ I put money into my savings account. ❻ I know I have to stop doing impulsive buying. ❼ I bought a car in 36-month installments. ❽ I struggle to pay on my credit card debt every month.

빈칸에 해당하는 표현을 채우며 한 번 더 복습해보세요.

먼저 만든 전체 문장을 떠올리며 빈칸을 채워보세요.

3rd step ★ 한 번 **더 더블**체크!

❶ You should ______ ______ ______ for retirement.
→ 돈을 마련해두다

❷ I wouldn't be able to maintain my current lifestyle if I ______ ______ ______ ______.
→ 소비를 줄이다

❸ I found out where I overspent by ______ ______ ______.
→ 소비내역을 추적함으로써
• by -ing ~함으로써

❹ I just ______ a few things ______ ______ ______ but where did all of my money go?
→ 여기저기서 샀다
• here and there 여기저기(서)

❺ I ______ ______ ______ my ______ ______.
→ 적금을 들다

❻ I know I have to stop ______ ______ ______.
→ 충동구매하는 것

❼ I ______ a car ______ 36-month ______.
→ ~을 할부로 사다

❽ I struggle to ______ ______ my ______ ______ ______ every month.
→ 카드 빚을 갚다

ANSWER ❶ set money aside ❷ cut back on spending ❸ tracking my spending ❹ bought, here and there ❺ put money into, savings account ❻ doing impulse buying ❼ bought, in, installments ❽ pay on, credit card debt

음원을 듣고 영어문장을 받아써보세요.

음원을 들으면서 원어민의 목소리를 성대모사하듯 입으로 소리내어 연습해보세요.

4th step ★ 최종점검! 영어문장 **받아써**보기 음원 듣기

❶ HINT retirement

❷ HINT maintain, current

❸ HINT overspent

❹ HINT bought

❺ HINT account

❻ HINT impulsive

❼ HINT installments

❽ HINT struggle, to

ANSWER ❶ You should set money aside for retirement. ❷ I wouldn't be able to maintain my current lifestyle if I cut back on spending. ❸ I found out where I overspent by tracking my spending. ❹ I just bought a few things here and there but where did all of my money go? ❺ I put money into my savings account. ❻ I know I have to stop doing impulsive buying. ❼ I bought a car in 36-month installments. ❽ I struggle to pay on my credit card debt every month.

day 39 돈 관리&재테크 2

신용 등급, 부동산 투자, 대출금 상환 등
돈 관리와 재테크에 관련된 표현입니다.

음원을 듣고 영어표현을 따라 말한 후, 손으로 써보세요.

1st step ★ 따라 **말**하고 **써**보며 표현 **익**히기

음원 듣기

❶ 생계를 꾸리다 ▸ make a living

❷ 재테크를 잘하다 ▸ be good at investing

❸ 돈을 벌다 ▸ make money

❹ 신용 등급이 높다/낮다 ▸ have a good/bad credit score

❺ 부동산에 투자하다 ▸ invest in real estate

❻ 주식에 투자하다 ▸ invest (money) in stocks

❼ 대출받다 ▸ get a loan

❽ 대출금을 상환하다 ▸ pay off the mortgage

앞에서 배운 표현을 떠올리며 한글에 해당하는 영어문장을 만들어보세요.

전체 문장을 만드는 게 어렵다면 오른쪽 옆 페이지를 참고하세요.

2nd step ★ 문장 속 표현 **확인**하기

❶ 일 그만 둔 후에, 가수 하면서 생계를 꾸리고 싶어.

❷ 내 생각에 그렉은 재테크를 잘하는 것 같아.

❸ 치킨 집 같은 소규모 창업을 해서 돈을 좀 벌려고 해.

❹ 신용등급이 낮으면, 대출받는 건 어렵지.

❺ 게일은 베트남 부동산에 투자해서 원금의 3배 수익이 났다고 들었어.

❻ 주식에 투자하는 것은 도박이나 똑같다고 봐.

❼ 낮은 이자로 대출을 받을 방법이 있을까?

❽ 우린 언제쯤 주택 대출금을 다 상환할 수 있을까?

ANSWER ❶ After quitting my job, I want to make a living as a singer. ❷ I think Greg is good at investing. ❸ I am planning to make money by opening a small business like a chicken place. ❹ Getting a loan is difficult when you have a bad credit score. ❺ I heard Gayle invested in real estate in Vietnam and made 3 times her original investment. ❻ I think investing in stocks is just like gambling. ❼ Are there any ways to get a loan with a low interest rate? ❽ When will we be able to pay off our mortgage?

빈칸에 해당하는 표현을 채우며 한 번 더 복습해보세요.

먼저 만든 전체 문장을 떠올리며 빈칸을 채워보세요.

3rd step ★ 한 번 **더 더블**체크!

❶ After quitting my job, I want to ______ as a singer.
→ 생계를 꾸리다

❷ I think Greg ______.
→ 재테크를 잘하다

❸ I am planning to ______ by opening a small business like a chicken place.
→ 돈을 벌다

❹ Getting a loan is difficult when you ______ a ______.
→ 신용등급이 높다/낮다

❺ I heard Gayle ______ in Vietnam and made 3 times her original investment.
→ 부동산에 투자했다

❻ I think ______ is just like gambling.
→ 주식에 투자하는 것

❼ Are there any ways to ______ with a low interest rate?
→ 대출받다

❽ When will we be able to ______ our ______?
→ 대출금을 상환하다

ANSWER ❶ make a living ❷ is good at investing ❸ make money ❹ have, bad credit score ❺ invested in real estate ❻ investing in stocks ❼ get a loan ❽ pay off, mortgage

음원을 듣고 영어문장을 받아써보세요.

음원을 들으면서 원어민의 목소리를 성대모사하듯 입으로 소리내어 연습해보세요.

4th step ★ 최종점검! 영어문장 **받아써**보기

음원 듣기 

❶ HINT quitting

❷ HINT investing

❸ HINT place

❹ HINT loan

❺ HINT estate, Vietnam

❻ HINT gambling

❼ HINT interest, rate

❽ HINT mortgage

ANSWER ❶ After quitting my job, I want to make a living as a singer. ❷ I think Greg is good at investing. ❸ I am planning to make money by opening a small business like a chicken place. ❹ Getting a loan is difficult when you have a bad credit score. ❺ I heard Gayle invested in real estate in Vietnam and made 3 times her original investment. ❻ I think investing in stocks is just like gambling. ❼ Are there any ways to get a loan with a low interest rate? ❽ When will we be able to pay off our mortgage?

day 40 차량 유지

차량 점검, 수리, 주유, 자동차 보험 들기 등
차량 유지와 관련된 표현입니다.

음원을 듣고 영어표현을 따라 말한 후, 손으로 써보세요.

1st step ★ 따라 **말**하고 **써**보며 표현 **익**히기

음원 듣기

❶ 차를 유지관리하다 ▸ maintain one's car

❷ 주차위반 딱지를 떼다 ▸ get a parking ticket

❸ 속도위반 딱지를 떼다 ▸ get a speeding ticket

❹ 연료를 채우다 ▸ fill one's car up with gas

❺ 자동차 보험에 들다 ▸ get car insurance

❻ 더 좋은 차로 업그레이드하다 ▸ upgrade to (B from A)

❼ 차를 점검하다 ▸ get one's car inspected

❽ 차 수리를 하다 ▸ get one's car repaired

앞에서 배운 표현을 떠올리며 한글에 해당하는 영어문장을 만들어보세요.

전체 문장을 만드는 게 어렵다면 오른쪽 옆 페이지를 참고하세요.

2nd step ★ 문장 속 표현 **확인**하기

❶ 차를 유지하는 데 돈이 많이 든다는 거 몰랐어?

❷ 너 버스 구역에 주차해서 주차 위반 딱지를 받았네.

❸ 집에 오는 길에 속도위반 딱지를 뗐어.

❹ 저 잠깐 주유소에 들러서 기름 좀 채울게요.

❺ 내가 자동차 보험 든 곳 알려줄게. 거기서 정말 싸게 할 수 있어.

❻ 저는 벤츠로 업그레이드해서 이 차를 파는 거예요.

❼ 얼마나 자주 차를 점검해야 하나요?

❽ 어디서 차 수리를 하시는지 여쭤봐도 될까요?

ANSWER ❶ Didn't you know it costs a lot to maintain your car? ❷ You got the parking ticket because you parked in the bus zone. ❸ I got a speeding ticket while driving home. ❹ I am stopping at the gas station to fill my car up with gas. ❺ I'll let you know where I got my car insurance. You can get the cheapest deal there. ❻ I'm selling this car because I upgraded to a Benz. ❼ How often do I have to get my car inspected? ❽ Can I ask where you get your car repaired?

빈칸에 해당하는 표현을 채우며 한 번 더 복습해보세요.

먼저 만든 전체 문장을 떠올리며 빈칸을 채워보세요.

3rd step ★ 한 번 **더 더블**체크!

❶ Didn't you know it costs a lot to ______________ ?
→ 차를 유지관리하다

❷ You ______ the ______________ because you parked in the bus zone.
→ 주차위반 딱지를 뗐다

❸ I ______________________ while driving home.
→ 속도위반 딱지를 뗐다

❹ I am stopping at the gas station to
______________________________ .
→ 연료를 채우다

❺ I'll let you know where I ______ my ______________ . You can get the cheapest deal there.
→ 자동차 보험에 들었다

❻ I'm selling this car because I ______________ a Benz.
→ 더 좋은 차로 업그레이드했다

❼ How often do I have to ______________________ ?
→ 차를 점검하다

❽ Can I ask where you ______ your ______________ ?
→ 차 수리를 하다

ANSWER ❶ maintain your car ❷ got, parking ticket ❸ got a speeding ticket ❹ fill my car up with gas ❺ got, car insurance ❻ upgraded to ❼ get my car inspected ❽ get, car repaired

음원을 듣고 영어문장을 받아써보세요.

음원을 들으면서 원어민의 목소리를 성대모사하듯 입으로 소리내어 연습해보세요.

4th step ★ 최종점검! 영어문장 **받아써**보기

음원 듣기 

❶ HINT maintain

❷ HINT zone

❸ HINT speeding

❹ HINT gas, station

❺ HINT insurance, deal

❻ HINT upgraded, Benz

❼ HINT inspected

❽ HINT repaired

ANSWER ❶ Didn't you know it costs a lot to maintain your car? ❷ You got the parking ticket because you parked in the bus zone. ❸ I got a speeding ticket while driving home. ❹ I am stopping at the gas station to fill my car up with gas. ❺ I'll let you know where I got my car insurance. You can get the cheapest deal there. ❻ I'm selling this car because I upgraded to a Benz. ❼ How often do I have to get my car inspected? ❽ Can I ask where you get your car repaired?

관리가 필요한 것들… 건강·돈·자동차

건강, 돈, 자동차 관리에 관련된 표현들로 이루어진 실제 대화에 도전!
음원을 들으며 영어문장을 따라 말해보세요.

음원 듣기

A After I pay for the bills and buy things here and there, there is nothing left in my bank account.

B Same here. I heard Gayle invested in real estate in Vietnam and made 3 times his original investment.

A He must be good at investing.

B Yes. He's really interested in how to best invest his money.

A I see. I put my money into my savings account.

B If you want to set aside more money for retirement, I think a savings account is not enough.

A 여러 대금 치르고, 여기 저기서 사고 나면, 내 계좌에 아무것도 안 남아.

B 나도 똑같아. 들어보니 게일은 베트남 부동산에 투자해서 원금의 3배 수익이 났다던데.

A 게일은 제테크를 잘하는구나.

B 응. 돈을 잘 투자하는 방법에 관심이 많아.

A 그렇구나. 나는 적금을 들고 있거든.

B 은퇴에 대비해 돈을 더 마련해두려면, 적금만으로는 부족한 것 같아.

week 09

대화를 시작하기 좋은 주제들, 스몰토크

day 41 나이

20대 중반, 30대 초반, 중년, 나이 차이 등 나이와 관련된 표현입니다.

음원을 듣고 영어표현을 따라 말한 후, 손으로 써보세요.

1st step ★ 따라 **말**하고 **써**보며 표현 **익**히기

음원 듣기

❶ 26살이다 ▶ be 26 years old

❷ 30대이다 ▶ be in one's 30s

❸ 30대 초반이다 ▶ be in one's early-30s

❹ 20대 중반이다 ▶ be in one's mid-20s

❺ 30대 후반이다 ▶ be in one's late-30s

❻ 중년이다 ▶ be middle-aged

❼ 나이보다 젊어 보이다 ▶ look younger than one's age

❽ 나이 차가 있다 ▶ have an age gap

앞에서 배운 표현을 떠올리며 한글에 해당하는 영어문장을 만들어보세요.

전체 문장을 만드는 게 어렵다면 오른쪽 옆 페이지를 참고하세요.

2nd step ★ 문장 속 표현 **확인**하기

❶ 그의 전 여자친구는 26살이었어.

❷ 30대에 할 수 있는 재미있는 것들이 정말 많아.

❸ 너 겨우 30대 초반이야. 왜 너 자신을 늙었다고 해?

❹ 나는 20대 중반이다.

❺ 내 남자친구는 30대 후반이야.

❻ 우리 아빠는 전형적인 중년 남성이다.

❼ 사라는 나이보다 젊어 보여.

❽ 내 남동생과 나는 나이 차가 좀 많이 나.

ANSWER ❶ His ex-girlfriend was 26 (years old). ❷ There are a lot of fun things to do in your 30s. ❸ You are only in your early-30s. Why are you calling yourself old? ❹ I am in my mid-20s. ❺ My boyfriend is in his late-30s. ❻ My dad is a typical middle-aged man. ❼ Sara looks younger than her age. ❽ There is a big age gap between me and my brother.

빈칸에 해당하는 표현을 채우며 한 번 더 복습해보세요.

먼저 만든 전체 문장을 떠올리며 빈칸을 채워보세요.

3rd step ★ 한 번 **더 더블**체크!

❶ His ex-girlfriend ______ ______ (years old).
→ 26살이었다

❷ There ______ a lot of fun things to do ______ your ______.
→ 30대이다
• 나이대 (초반/중반/후반)의: be in one's (early/mid/late) 30s

❸ You ______ only ______ ______ ______. Why are you calling yourself old?
→ 30대 초반이다

❹ I ______ ______ ______ ______.
→ 20대 중반이다

❺ My boyfriend ______ ______ ______ ______.
→ 30대 후반이다

❻ My dad ______ a typical ______ man.
→ 중년이다

❼ Sara ______ ______ ______ ______ ______.
→ 나이보다 젊어 보이다

❽ There is a big ______ ______ between me and my brother.
→ 나이 차가 있다

ANSWER ❶ was 26 ❷ are, in, 30s ❸ are, in your early-30s ❹ am in my mid-20s ❺ is in his late-30s ❻ is, middle-aged ❼ looks younger than her age ❽ age gap

음원을 듣고 영어문장을 받아써보세요.

음원을 들으면서 원어민의 목소리를 성대모사하듯 입으로 소리내어 연습해보세요.

4th step ★ 최종점검! 영어문장 **받아써**보기 음원 듣기

❶ HINT ex-girlfriend

❷ HINT fun

❸ HINT early-30s

❹ HINT mid-20s

❺ HINT late-30s

❻ HINT typical

❼ HINT younger

❽ HINT age, gap

ANSWER ❶ His ex-girlfriend was 26 (years old). ❷ There are a lot of fun things to do in your 30s. ❸ You are only in your early-30s. Why are you calling yourself old? ❹ I am in my mid-20s. ❺ My boyfriend is in his late-30s. ❻ My dad is a typical middle-aged man. ❼ Sara looks younger than her age. ❽ There is a big age gap between me and my brother.

day 42 날씨

비가 오고, 미세 먼지 농도가 높고, 습기가 많은 등 날씨와 관련된 표현입니다.

음원을 듣고 영어표현을 따라 말한 후, 손으로 써보세요.

1st step ★ 따라 **말**하고 **써**보며 표현 **익**히기

음원 듣기

❶ 미세먼지 농도가 높다 ▸ fine dust level is high

❷ 비가 오다 ▸ rain

❸ 맑다 ▸ be clear

❹ 습기가 많다 ▸ be humid

❺ 쌀쌀하다 ▸ be chilly

❻ (얼음이 얼 것처럼) 매우 춥다 ▸ be freezing

❼ (일반적으로) 눈 오는 날에는 ▸ on a snowy day

❽ (일반적으로) 더운 날에는 ▸ on a hot day

앞에서 배운 표현을 떠올리며 한글에 해당하는 영어문장을 만들어보세요.

전체 문장을 만드는 게 어렵다면 오른쪽 옆 페이지를 참고하세요.

2nd step ★ 문장 속 표현 **확인**하기

❶ 웬만하면 밖에 나가지 마세요. 미세먼지 농도가 높아요.

❷ 비가 올 것 같아.

❸ 내일은 하늘이 맑을 거야.

❹ 여름에는 너무 습해서 밖에 나가고 싶지 않아.

❺ 좀 쌀쌀하네. 그냥 집에 있을까 봐.

❻ 밖이 엄청 추워. 단단히 챙겨 입어.

❼ 눈 오는 날에는 교통 체증이 엄청 심해요.

❽ 나는 더운 날에는 콜라를 두세 캔씩 마시는 것 같아.

ANSWER ❶ Please try not to go outside. The fine dust level is high. ❷ It looks like it is going to rain. ❸ The sky will be clear tomorrow. ❹ It is so humid in the summer that I don't want to go outside. ❺ It is a little chilly. I think I'll just stay home. ❻ It is freezing outside. Be sure to bundle up. ❼ On a snowy day, there is a lot of traffic. ❽ On a hot day, I think I drink two or three cans of coke.

빈칸에 해당하는 표현을 채우며 한 번 더 복습해보세요.

먼저 만든 전체 문장을 떠올리며 빈칸을 채워보세요.

3rd step ★ 한 번 **더 더블**체크!

❶ Please try not to go outside. The ________ ________ ________ ________ ________.
→ 미세먼지 농도가 높다

❷ It looks like it is going to ________.
→ 비 오다

❸ The sky will ________ ________ tomorrow.
→ 맑다

❹ It ________ so ________ in the summer that I don't want to go outside.
→ 습기가 많다

❺ It ________ a little ________. I think I'll just stay home.
→ 쌀쌀하다

❻ It ________ ________ outside. Be sure to bundle up.
→ (얼음이 얼 것처럼) 매우 춥다

• bundle up (추위를 피하기 위해) 단단히 챙겨 입다

❼ ________ ________ ________ ________, there is a lot of traffic.
→ 눈 오는 날에는

❽ ________ ________ ________ ________, I think I drink two or three cans of coke.
→ 더운 날에는

ANSWER ❶ fine dust level is high ❷ rain ❸ be clear ❹ is, humid ❺ is, chilly ❻ is freezing ❼ On a snowy day ❽ On a hot day

음원을 듣고 영어문장을 받아써보세요.

음원을 들으면서 원어민의 목소리를 성대모사하듯
입으로 소리내어 연습해보세요.

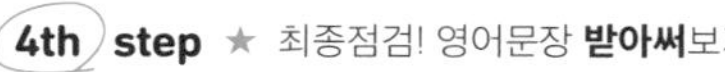

4th step ★ 최종점검! 영어문장 **받아써**보기 음원 듣기

❶ HINT fine, dust

❷ HINT going

❸ HINT clear

❹ HINT humid

❺ HINT chilly

❻ HINT freezing, bundle

❼ HINT traffic

❽ HINT coke

ANSWER ❶ Please try not to go outside. The fine dust level is high. ❷ It looks like it is going to rain. ❸ The sky will be clear tomorrow. ❹ It is so humid in the summer that I don't want to go outside. ❺ It is a little chilly. I think I'll just stay home. ❻ It is freezing outside. Be sure to bundle up. ❼ On a snowy day, there is a lot of traffic. ❽ On a hot day, I think I drink two or three cans of coke.

day 43 육아&자녀교육

출산, 아기 돌보기, 육아 휴직 등
육아와 자녀교육에 관련된 표현입니다.

음원을 듣고 영어표현을 따라 말한 후, 손으로 써보세요.

1st step ★ 따라 **말**하고 **써**보며 표현 **익**히기

음원 듣기

❶ 아기를 출산하다 ▸ give birth to a baby

❷ 아이를 기르다[돌보다] ▸ raise[take care of] children

❸ 모유 수유하다 ▸ breast-feed one's baby

❹ 분유를 먹이다 ▸ bottle-feed one's baby

❺ 아기를 먹이다 ▸ feed one's baby

❻ 기저귀를 갈다 ▸ change the diaper

❼ 학교/유치원에 보내다 ▸ send one's children to school/kindergarten

❽ 육아 휴직을 하다 ▸ take maternity leave

앞에서 배운 표현을 떠올리며 한글에 해당하는 영어문장을 만들어보세요.

전체 문장을 만드는 게 어렵다면 오른쪽 옆 페이지를 참고하세요.

2nd step ★ 문장 속 표현 **확인**하기

❶ 나라가 아들을 나았어!

❷ 아이들 기르는 게 내가 해본 일 중에 가장 어려운 것 같아.

❸ 모유 수유하셨어요?

❹ 아니요, 모유가 안 나와서 분유 먹여야 했어요.

❺ 남편이 아기들을 먹여줘요.

❻ 아이쿠, 냄새. 기저귀 갈 시간이네!

❼ 한국에서는 8살에 아이들을 학교에 보내요.

❽ 저는 육아휴직 중이에요.

ANSWER ❶ Nara gave birth to a baby boy! ❷ Raising children seems to be the most difficult thing I've ever done. ❸ Did you breast-feed your babies? ❹ No, I couldn't produce any breast milk so I had to bottle-feed them. ❺ My husband feeds our babies. ❻ Oh, you stink. Time to change your diaper! ❼ In Korea, we send our children to school at the age of 8. ❽ I am taking maternity leave.

빈칸에 해당하는 표현을 채우며 한 번 더 복습해보세요.

먼저 만든 전체 문장을 떠올리며 빈칸을 채워보세요.

3rd step ★ 한 번 **더 더블**체크!

❶ Nara ______ ______ ______ ______ ______ boy!
→ 아기를 출산했다

❷ ______ ______ seems to be the most difficult thing I've ever done.
→ 아이들을 기르는 것

❸ Did you ______ ______ ______ ?
→ 아기들을 모유 수유하다

❹ No, I couldn't produce any breast milk so I had to ______ them.
→ 분유를 먹이다

❺ My husband ______ ______ ______ .
→ 우리 아기들을 먹이다

❻ Oh, you stink. Time to ______ your ______ !
→ 기저귀를 갈다

❼ In Korea, we ______ ______ ______ ______ ______ at the age of 8.
→ 아이들을 학교에 보내다

❽ I am ______ ______ ______ .
→ 육아 휴직 중이다

ANSWER ❶ gave birth to a baby ❷ Raising children ❸ breast-feed your babies ❹ bottle-feed ❺ feed our babies ❻ change, diaper ❼ send our children to school ❽ taking maternity leave

음원을 듣고 영어문장을 받아써보세요.

음원을 들으면서 원어민의 목소리를 성대모사하듯 입으로 소리내어 연습해보세요.

음원 듣기 

❶ HINT gave, birth

❷ HINT raising

❸ HINT breast-feed

❹ HINT bottle-feed

❺ HINT feeds

❻ HINT stink, diaper

❼ HINT age

❽ HINT maternity

ANSWER ❶ Nara gave birth to a baby boy! ❷ Raising children seems to be the most difficult thing I've ever done. ❸ Did you breast-feed your babies? ❹ No, I couldn't produce any breast milk so I had to bottle-feed them. ❺ My husband feeds our babies. ❻ Oh, you stink. Time to change your diaper! ❼ In Korea, we send our children to school at the age of 8. ❽ I am taking maternity leave.

day 44 최신 영화

영화 상영, 개봉, 영화 추천, 주연 등
영화에 관련된 표현입니다.

음원을 듣고 영어표현을 따라 말한 후, 손으로 써보세요.

1st step ★ 따라 **말**하고 **써**보며 표현 **익**히기

음원 듣기

❶ 개봉하다 ▸ be released

❷ 상영 중이다 ▸ be showing

❸ 영화를 추천하다 ▸ recommend a movie

❹ 영화에 출연하다 ▸ star in the movie

❺ 주연을 맡다 ▸ play the lead role

❻ 조연을 맡다 ▸ play a supporting role

❼ 실화를 바탕으로 하다 ▸ be based on a true story

❽ ~에 안목이 있다 ▸ have a good taste in ~

앞에서 배운 표현을 떠올리며 한글에 해당하는 영어문장을 만들어보세요.

전체 문장을 만드는 게 어렵다면 오른쪽 옆 페이지를 참고하세요.

2nd step ★ 문장 속 표현 **확인**하기

❶ 그 영화 지난주에 개봉했어요.

❷ 그 영화 CGV에서 아직 상영 중이에요.

❸ 영화 〈블랙팬서〉 보셨어요? 추천하세요?

❹ 유해진이 영화 〈택시 운전사〉에 출연했어요.

❺ 송강호가 그 영화에서 주연을 맡았어요.

❻ 류준열이 그 영화에서 조연을 맡았어요.

❼ 〈택시 운전사〉는 실화를 기반으로 한 영화에요.

❽ 당신은 영화 보는 안목이 있으시군요.

ANSWER ❶ The movie was released last week. ❷ The movie is still showing at CGV. ❸ Have you seen the movie '*Black Panther*'? Do you recommend it? ❹ Yoo Hae-jin starred in the movie '*Taxi Driver*'. ❺ Song Kang-ho played the lead role in the movie. ❻ Ryu Jun-yeol played a supporting role in the movie. ❼ '*Taxi Driver*' is based on a true story. ❽ You have good taste in movies.

빈칸에 해당하는 표현을 채우며 한 번 더 복습해보세요.

먼저 만든 전체 문장을 떠올리며 빈칸을 채워보세요.

3rd step ★ 한 번 **더 더블**체크!

❶ The movie ________ ________ last week.
→ 개봉했다

❷ The movie ________ still ________ at CGV.
→ 영화가 상영 중이다

❸ Have you seen the movie *'Black Panther'*? Do you ________ it?
→ 영화를 추천하다

❹ Yoo Hae-jin ________ ________ ________ ________ *'Taxi Driver'*.
→ 영화에 출연했다

❺ Song Kang-ho ________ ________ ________ ________ in the movie.
→ 주연을 맡았다

❻ Ryu Jun-yeol ________ ________ ________ ________ in the movie.
→ 조연을 맡았다

❼ *'Taxi Driver'* ________ ________ ________ ________ ________ ________ .
→ 실제 이야기를 바탕으로 하다

❽ You ________ ________ ________ ________ movies.
→ ~에 안목이 있다

ANSWER ❶ was released ❷ is, showing ❸ recommend ❹ starred in the movie ❺ played the lead role ❻ played a supporting role ❼ is based on a true story ❽ have good taste in

음원을 듣고 영어문장을 받아써보세요.

음원을 들으면서 원어민의 목소리를 성대모사하듯 입으로 소리내어 연습해보세요.

4th step ★ 최종점검! 영어문장 **받아써**보기

음원 듣기 

❶ HINT released

❷ HINT showing

❸ HINT recommend

❹ HINT starred

❺ HINT lead, role

❻ HINT supporting

❼ HINT based, on

❽ HINT taste

ANSWER ❶ The movie was released last week. ❷ The movie is still showing at CGV. ❸ Have you seen the movie '*Black Panther*'? Do you recommend it? ❹ Yoo Hae-jin starred in the movie '*Taxi Driver*'. ❺ Song Kang-ho played the lead role in the movie. ❻ Ryu Jun-yeol played a supporting role in the movie. ❼ '*Taxi Driver*' is based on a true story. ❽ You have good taste in movies.

day 45 기간 표현

하루 종일, 여름 내내, 밤새도록 등 기간에 관련된 표현입니다.

음원을 듣고 영어표현을 따라 말한 후, 손으로 써보세요.

1st step ★ 따라 **말**하고 **써**보며 표현 **익**히기

음원 듣기

❶ 한낮에 ▸ in the middle of the day

❷ 한밤중에 ▸ in the middle of the night

❸ 한여름에/한겨울에 ▸ in the middle of summer/winter

❹ 뭔가를 하던 중에 ▸ in the middle of something

❺ 하루 종일 / 한 주 내내 ▸ all day/week (long)

❻ 아침 내내 ▸ all morning

❼ 밤새도록 ▸ all night

❽ 겨울/여름 내내 ▸ all winter/summer

앞에서 배운 표현을 떠올리며 한글에 해당하는 영어문장을 만들어보세요.

전체 문장을 만드는 게 어렵다면 오른쪽 옆 페이지를 참고하세요.

2nd step ★ 문장 속 표현 **확인**하기

❶ 낮술 어때?

❷ 학수가 한밤중에 나를 깨웠어.

❸ 한국에서 한여름에는 정말 덥고 습해요.

❹ 나 뭐하던 중이라 전화를 못 받았어.

❺ 나 오늘 하루 종일 바빴어.

❻ 아침 내내 집안일하며 보냈어.

❼ 나는 밤새도록 그를 기다렸어.

❽ 겨울 내내 사업이 잘 안 됐어요.

ANSWER ❶ How about a drink in the middle of the day? ❷ Haksoo woke me up in the middle of the night. ❸ It's really hot and humid in the middle of summer in Korea. ❹ I was in the middle of something so I couldn't take your call. ❺ I have been busy all day long. ❻ I spent all morning doing house chores. ❼ I have waited for him all night. ❽ Business was slow all winter.

빈칸에 해당하는 표현을 채우며 한 번 더 복습해보세요.

먼저 만든 전체 문장을 떠올리며 빈칸을 채워보세요.

3rd step ★ 한 번 **더 더블**체크!

❶ How about a drink ______________________________ ?
→ 한낮에

❷ Haksoo woke me up ______________________________ .
→ 한밤중에

❸ It's really hot and humid ______________________________ in Korea.
→ 한여름에

❹ I was ______________________________ so I couldn't take your call.
→ 뭔가를 하던 중에

❺ I have been busy ____________________ .
→ 하루 종일

❻ I spent ______________ doing house chores.
→ 아침 내내

❼ I have waited for him ______________ .
→ 밤새도록

❽ Business was slow ______________ .
→ 겨울 내내

ANSWER ❶ in the middle of the day ❷ in the middle of the night ❸ in the middle of summer ❹ in the middle of something ❺ all day long ❻ all morning ❼ all night ❽ all winter

음원을 듣고 영어문장을 받아써보세요.

음원을 들으면서 원어민의 목소리를 성대모사하듯 입으로 소리내어 연습해보세요.

4th step ★ 최종점검! 영어문장 **받아써**보기

음원 듣기 

❶ HINT middle

❷ HINT woke, up

❸ HINT humid

❹ HINT something

❺ HINT busy

❻ HINT house, chores

❼ HINT waited

❽ HINT slow

ANSWER ❶ How about a drink in the middle of the day? ❷ Haksoo woke me up in the middle of the night. ❸ It's really hot and humid in the middle of summer in Korea. ❹ I was in the middle of something so I couldn't take your call. ❺ I have been busy all day long. ❻ I spent all morning doing house chores. ❼ I have waited for him all night. ❽ Business was slow all winter.

대화를 시작하기 좋은 주제들

스몰토크에 관련된 표현들로 이루어진 실제 대화에 도전!
음원을 들으며 영어문장을 따라 말해보세요.

음원 듣기

A Sorry, I was in the middle of doing something so I couldn't take your call.

B You must be busy right now. How about we watch a movie at my place later?

A On a hot day like this, a good movie is perfect! What are we watching tonight?

B '*American Hustle*'. Christian Bale played the lead role in the movie.

A I wanted to watch it! You have good taste in movies. Have you asked Minji?

B I haven't asked her because I thought she would be busy taking care of her babies.

A 미안, 나 뭐 좀 하던 중이라 네 전화를 못 받았어.

B 지금 바쁜가보네. 이따 우리 집에서 괜찮은 영화 한 편 보는 거 어때?

A 이렇게 더운 날엔, 괜찮은 영화 한 편 최고지! 오늘 무슨 영화 볼까?

B 〈아메리칸 허슬〉. 크리스찬 베일이 그 영화에서 주연을 맡았어.

A 나 그거 보고 싶었어! 네가 영화 보는 안목이 있다니까. 민지한테는 물어봤어?

B 애기들 보느라 바쁠 것 같아서 안 물어봤어.

week 10

반대가 끌리는 이유! 짝꿍 동사구

day 46 짝꿍 동사구 1

접다/펴다, 데우다/식히다 등
반대의 뜻을 가진 짝꿍 동사에 관련된 표현입니다.

음원을 듣고 영어표현을 따라 말한 후, 손으로 써보세요.

1st step ★ 따라 **말**하고 **써**보며 표현 **익**히기

음원 듣기

1. 접다 ▸ fold
2. 펴다 ▸ unfold
3. 짐을 싸다 ▸ pack
4. (쌓았던 짐을) 풀다 ▸ unpack
5. 묶다 ▸ tie
6. (묶은 것을) 풀다 ▸ untie
7. 데우다 ▸ heat up
8. 식히다 ▸ cool off

앞에서 배운 표현을 떠올리며 한글에 해당하는 영어문장을 만들어보세요.

전체 문장을 만드는 게 어렵다면 오른쪽 옆 페이지를 참고하세요.

2nd step ★ 문장 속 표현 **확인**하기

❶ 옷을 가지런하게 접으세요.

❷ 종이를 펴세요.

❸ 짐 쌌어?

❹ 짐은 다 푸셨어요?

❺ 나 어때 보여? 오늘은 머리를 묶어봤어.

❻ 어, 너 신발끈 풀렸어.

❼ 전자레인지에 이거 좀 데워주시겠어요?

❽ 이 쿠키들을 식히는 데 1분 정도 걸릴 거예요.

ANSWER ❶ Fold the clothes neatly. ❷ Unfold the paper. ❸ Did you pack? ❹ Did you unpack? ❺ How do I look? I tied my hair up today. ❻ Hey, your shoe is untied. ❼ Could you heat this food up in the microwave? ❽ The cookies will take a minute to cool off.

빈칸에 해당하는 표현을 채우며 한 번 더 복습해보세요.

먼저 만든 전체 문장을 떠올리며 빈칸을 채워보세요.

3rd step ★ 한 번 **더 더블**체크!

❶ ________ the clothes neatly.
→ 접다

❷ ________ the paper.
→ 펴다

❸ Did you ________ ?
→ 짐을 싸다

❹ Did you ________ ?
→ (쌓았던 짐을) 풀다

❺ How do I look? I ________ my hair up today.
→ 묶었다

❻ Hey, your shoe is ________ .
→ (묶은 것을) 풀었다

❼ Could you ________ this food ________ in the microwave?
→ 데우다

❽ The cookies will take a minute to ________ .
→ 식히다

ANSWER ❶ Fold ❷ Unfold ❸ pack ❹ unpack ❺ tied ❻ untied ❼ heat, up ❽ cool off

음원을 듣고 영어문장을 받아써보세요.

음원을 들으면서 원어민의 목소리를 성대모사하듯
입으로 소리내어 연습해보세요.

4th step ★ 최종점검! 영어문장 **받아써**보기 음원 듣기

❶ HINT neatly

❷ HINT unfold

❸ HINT pack

❹ HINT unpack

❺ HINT hair

❻ HINT shoe

❼ HINT microwave

❽ HINT minute

ANSWER ❶ Fold the clothes neatly. ❷ Unfold the paper. ❸ Did you pack? ❹ Did you unpack? ❺ How do I look? I tied my hair up today. ❻ Hey, your shoe is untied. ❼ Could you heat this food up in the microwave? ❽ The cookies will take a minute to cool off.

day 47 짝꿍 동사구 2

다투다/화해하다, 존경하다/무시하다 등
반대의 뜻을 가진 짝꿍 동사에 관련된 표현입니다.

음원을 듣고 영어표현을 따라 말한 후, 손으로 써보세요.

1st step ★ 따라 **말**하고 **써**보며 표현 **익**히기

음원 듣기

❶ 오해를 사다 ▸ cause a misunderstanding

❷ 오해를 풀다 ▸ resolve a misunderstanding

❸ ~와 말다툼하다 ▸ argue with ~

❹ ~와 화해하다 ▸ make up with ~

❺ 스트레스를 받다 ▸ be stressed out

❻ 스트레스를 풀다 ▸ relieve stress

❼ ~를 존경하다 ▸ look up to ~

❽ ~를 무시하다 ▸ look down on ~

앞에서 배운 표현을 떠올리며 한글에 해당하는 영어문장을 만들어보세요.

전체 문장을 만드는 게 어렵다면 오른쪽 옆 페이지를 참고하세요.

2nd step ★ 문장 속 표현 **확인**하기

❶ 제가 오해를 샀다면 죄송합니다.

❷ 만나서 얘기하죠. 그래야 오해가 풀릴 것 같습니다.

❸ 나 지난주에 남자친구와 다퉜어.

❹ 그 사람이 결국 '미안하다'고 해서 우리 화해했어요.

❺ 나 직장에서 스트레스 받아.

❻ 스트레스를 푸는 방법에 대한 팁 좀 주세요.

❼ 저는 제 아버지를 존경해요.

❽ 그녀는 그것 때문에 나를 좀 무시해.

ANSWER ❶ I am sorry for the misunderstanding I may have caused. ❷ Let's meet and talk. That will help resolve the misunderstanding. ❸ I argued with my boyfriend last week. ❹ We made up because he finally said "sorry". ❺ I am stressed out at work. ❻ Please give me some tips on how to relieve stress. ❼ I look up to my father. ❽ She looks down on me because of that.

빈칸에 해당하는 표현을 채우며 한 번 더 복습해보세요.

먼저 만든 전체 문장을 떠올리며 빈칸을 채워보세요.

3rd step ★ 한 번 **더 더블**체크!

❶ I am sorry for the ______ I may have ______ .
→ 오해를 했다

❷ Let's meet and talk. That will help ______ the ______ .
→ 오해를 풀다

❸ I ______ ______ my boyfriend last week.
→ ~와 말다툼했다

❹ We ______ ______ because he finally said "sorry".
→ ~와 화해했다

❺ I ______ ______ ______ at work.
→ 스트레스를 받다

❻ Please give me some tips on how to ______ ______ .
→ 스트레스를 풀다

❼ I ______ ______ ______ my father.
→ ~를 존경하다

❽ She ______ ______ ______ me because of that.
→ ~를 무시하다

ANSWER ❶ misunderstanding, caused ❷ resolve, misunderstanding ❸ argued with ❹ made up ❺ am stressed out ❻ relieve stress ❼ look up to ❽ looks down on

음원을 듣고 영어문장을 받아써보세요.

음원을 들으면서 원어민의 목소리를 성대모사하듯 입으로 소리내어 연습해보세요.

4th step ★ 최종점검! 영어문장 **받아써**보기

음원 듣기 

❶ HINT caused

❷ HINT resolve

❸ HINT argued

❹ HINT finally

❺ HINT stressed

❻ HINT relieve

❼ HINT father

❽ HINT because

ANSWER ❶ I am sorry for the misunderstanding I may have caused. ❷ Let's meet and talk. That will help resolve the misunderstanding. ❸ I argued with my boyfriend last week. ❹ We made up because he finally said "sorry". ❺ I am stressed out at work. ❻ Please give me some tips on how to relieve stress. ❼ I look up to my father. ❽ She looks down on me because of that.

짝꿍 동사구 3

분해하다/조립하다, 합격하다/떨어지다 등
반대의 뜻을 가진 짝꿍 동사에 관련된 표현입니다.

음원을 듣고 영어표현을 따라 말한 후, 손으로 써보세요.

1st step ★ 따라 **말**하고 **써**보며 표현 **익**히기

음원 듣기

1. 싸게 사다 ▸ get a good deal on
2. 비싸게 사다 ▸ get a bad deal on
3. 분해하다 ▸ take apart
4. 조립하다 ▸ put together
5. 시험에 합격하다 ▸ pass the exam
6. 시험에 떨어지다 ▸ fail the exam
7. 과대평가하다 ▸ overestimate/overrate
8. 과소평가하다 ▸ underestimate/underrate

앞에서 배운 표현을 떠올리며 한글에 해당하는 영어문장을 만들어보세요.

전체 문장을 만드는 게 어렵다면 오른쪽 옆 페이지를 참고하세요.

2nd step ★ 문장 속 표현 **확인**하기

❶ 나 이 가방 싸게 잘 샀어.

❷ 이 차 좀 비싸게 주고 샀어.

❸ 나는 컴퓨터 분해하는 것을 좋아해.

❹ 그것들 다 조립하는 데 시간이 얼마나 걸렸어요?

❺ 저 결국 시험에 합격했어요.

❻ 네가 시험에 떨어진 게 놀랍지는 않은데.

❼ 그의 능력은 매우 과대평가됐다고 봐.

❽ 이 브랜드는 꽤 과소평가되었어. 나는 더 지불할 의사도 있어.

ANSWER ❶ I got a good deal on the bag. ❷ I got a bad deal on the car. ❸ I like to take computers apart. ❹ How long did it take to put them all together? ❺ I finally passed the exam. ❻ No wonder you failed the exam. ❼ I think his skills are highly overrated. ❽ This brand is quite underrated. I would be willing to pay more.

빈칸에 해당하는 표현을 채우며 한 번 더 복습해보세요.

먼저 만든 전체 문장을 떠올리며 빈칸을 채워보세요.

3rd step ★ 한 번 **더 더블**체크!

❶ I ______ on the bag.
→ 싸게 샀다

❷ I ______ on the car.
→ 비싸게 사다

❸ I like to ______ computers ______ .
→ 분해하다

❹ How long did it take to ______ them all ______ ?
→ 조립하다

❺ I finally ______ .
→ 시험에 합격했다

❻ No wonder you ______ .
→ 시험에 떨어졌다

❼ I think his skills are highly ______ .
→ 과대평가되었다

❽ This brand is quite ______ . I would be willing to pay more.
→ 과소평가되었다

ANSWER ❶ got a good deal ❷ got a bad deal ❸ take, apart ❹ put, together ❺ passed the exam ❻ failed the exam ❼ overrated ❽ underrated

음원을 듣고 영어문장을 받아써보세요.

음원을 들으면서 원어민의 목소리를 성대모사하듯 입으로 소리내어 연습해보세요.

4th step ★ 최종점검! 영어문장 **받아써**보기 음원 듣기

❶ HINT deal

❷ HINT on

❸ HINT apart

❹ HINT together

❺ HINT finally

❻ HINT wonder

❼ HINT highly

❽ HINT quite, willing

ANSWER ❶ I got a good deal on the bag. ❷ I got a bad deal on the car. ❸ I like to take computers apart. ❹ How long did it take to put them all together? ❺ I finally passed the exam. ❻ No wonder you failed the exam. ❼ I think his skills are highly overrated. ❽ This brand is quite underrated. I would be willing to pay more.

day 49 짝꿍 동사구 4

시동을 걸다/끄다, 속도를 내다/줄이다 등 반대의 뜻을 가진 짝꿍 동사에 관련된 표현입니다.

음원을 듣고 영어표현을 따라 말한 후, 손으로 써보세요.

1st step ★ 따라 **말**하고 **써**보며 표현 **익**히기

음원 듣기

1. ~을 습관화하다 ▶ make a habit of ~
2. ~의 습관을 없애다 ▶ break the habit of ~
3. (자동차) 시동을 걸다 ▶ start the car
4. (자동차) 시동을 끄다 ▶ stop the engine
5. 속도를 내다 ▶ speed up
6. 속도를 줄이다 ▶ slow down
7. 최대화하다 ▶ maximize
8. 최소화하다 ▶ minimize

앞에서 배운 표현을 떠올리며 한글에 해당하는 영어문장을 만들어보세요.

전체 문장을 만드는 게 어렵다면 오른쪽 옆 페이지를 참고하세요.

2nd step ★ 문장 속 표현 **확인**하기

❶ 너는 건강한 음식을 먹는 걸 습관화하는 게 좋겠어.

❷ 너 정크푸드 먹는 습관을 버리는 게 좋겠어.

❸ 차 시동이 안 걸려.

❹ 주유하는 동안에는 시동을 꺼주세요.

❺ 우리 마감 기한 맞추려면 속도를 좀 내야겠어요.

❻ 우리는 어떻게 천천히 살면서 삶을 즐길 수 있는지를 배울 필요가 있어.

❼ 가능성을 제한하지 말고 당신의 잠재력을 최대화하세요.

❽ 직장에서는 너의 약점을 최소화해야 해.

ANSWER ❶ You should make a habit of eating healthy food. ❷ You should break the habit of eating junk food. ❸ I can't start the car. ❹ Please stop the engine while filling the car up with gas. ❺ We need to speed up to meet the deadline. ❻ We need to learn how to slow down and enjoy our lives. ❼ You shouldn't limit your possibilities, but maximize your potential. ❽ You should minimize your weak points at work.

빈칸에 해당하는 표현을 채우며 한 번 더 복습해보세요.

먼저 만든 전체 문장을 떠올리며 빈칸을 채워보세요.

3rd step ★ 한 번 **더 더블**체크!

❶ You should ______________ eating healthy food.
→ ~을 습관화하다

❷ You should ______________ eating junk food.
→ ~의 습관을 없애다

❸ I can't ______________ .
→ 시동을 걸다

❹ Please ______________ while filling the car up with gas.
→ 시동을 끄다

❺ We need to ______________ to meet the deadline.
→ 속도를 내다

❻ We need to learn how to ______________ and enjoy our lives.
→ 속도를 줄이다

❼ You shouldn't limit your possibilities, but ______________ your potential.
→ 최대화하다

❽ You should ______________ your weak points at work.
→ 최소화하다

ANSWER ❶ make a habit of ❷ break the habit of ❸ start the car ❹ stop the engine ❺ speed up ❻ slow down ❼ maximize ❽ minimize

음원을 듣고 영어문장을 받아써보세요.

음원을 들으면서 원어민의 목소리를 성대모사하듯
입으로 소리내어 연습해보세요.

4th step ★ 최종점검! 영어문장 **받아써**보기 음원 듣기

❶ HINT habit

❷ HINT junk

❸ HINT start

❹ HINT engine

❺ HINT deadline

❻ HINT enjoy

❼ HINT potential

❽ HINT weak, points

ANSWER ❶ You should make a habit of eating healthy food. ❷ You should break the habit of eating junk food. ❸ I can't start the car. ❹ Please stop the engine while filling the car up with gas. ❺ We need to speed up to meet the deadline. ❻ We need to learn how to slow down and enjoy our lives. ❼ You shouldn't limit your possibilities, but maximize your potential. ❽ You should minimize your weak points at work.

짝꿍 동사구 5

차려입다/편하게 입다, 껴주다/빼주다 등
반대의 뜻을 가진 짝꿍 동사에 관련된 표현입니다.

음원을 듣고 영어표현을 따라 말한 후, 손으로 써보세요.

1st step ★ 따라 **말**하고 **써**보며 표현 **익**히기

음원 듣기

❶ 차려입다 ▶ dress up

❷ 편안하게 입다 ▶ dress down

❸ ~도 껴주다 ▶ count ~ in

❹ ~는 빼주다 ▶ count ~ out

❺ 줄 서서 기다리다 ▶ wait in line

❻ 새치기하다 ▶ cut in line

❼ 연결하다 ▶ connect

❽ 연결을 해제하다 ▶ disconnect

앞에서 배운 표현을 떠올리며 한글에 해당하는 영어문장을 만들어보세요.

전체 문장을 만드는 게 어렵다면 오른쪽 옆 페이지를 참고하세요.

2nd step ★ 문장 속 표현 **확인**하기

❶ 그 파티에 그렇게 빼입을 필요는 없어.

❷ '노 타이 데이'에 사람들은 넥타이를 풀고 편안하게 입어.

❸ 그 저녁 모임에 저도 껴주세요!

❹ 초대해줘서 감사한데 이번에 저는 빼주세요. 지금 너무 바빠서요.

❺ 서둘러, 사라가 레스토랑에서 우리를 위해 줄 서서 기다리고 있어.

❻ 새치기는 매너가 없는 거지.

❼ 지하철이 HS빌딩과 연결되어 있어. 찾을 수 있을 거야.

❽ 부품을 제거하기 전에 케이블 연결을 반드시 해제하세요.

ANSWER ❶ You don't need to dress up for the party. ❷ On 'no-tie' days, people take off their ties and dress down. ❸ You can count me in for the dinner! ❹ Thanks for the invitation, but count me out this time. I am too busy at the moment. ❺ Hurry, Sara is waiting in line for us at the restaurant. ❻ Cutting in line is bad manners. ❼ The subway is connected to the HS building. You won't miss it. ❽ Make sure you disconnect the cable before removing the component.

빈칸에 해당하는 표현을 채우며 한 번 더 복습해보세요.

먼저 만든 전체 문장을 떠올리며 빈칸을 채워보세요.

3rd step ★ 한 번 **더 더블**체크!

❶ You don't need to ______ ______ for the party.
→ 차려입다

❷ On 'no-tie' days, people take off their ties and ______ ______.
→ 편안하게 입다

❸ You can ______ me ______ for the dinner!
→ 껴주세요

❹ Thanks for the invitation, but ______ me ______ this time. I am too busy at the moment.
→ 빼주세요

❺ Hurry, Sara is ______ ______ ______ for us at the restaurant.
→ 줄 서서 기다리고 있다

❻ ______ ______ ______ is bad manners.
→ 새치기하는 것

❼ The subway is ______ to the HS building. You won't miss it.
→ 연결되었다

❽ Make sure you ______ the cable before removing the component.
→ 연결을 해제하다

ANSWER ❶ dress up ❷ dress down ❸ count, in ❹ count, out ❺ waiting in line ❻ Cutting in line ❼ connected ❽ disconnect

음원을 듣고 영어문장을 받아써보세요.

음원을 들으면서 원어민의 목소리를 성대모사하듯 입으로 소리내어 연습해보세요.

★ 최종점검! 영어문장 **받아써**보기

음원 듣기 

❶ HINT need

❷ HINT no-tie, days

❸ HINT count

❹ HINT moment

❺ HINT restaurant

❻ HINT manners

❼ HINT subway

❽ HINT component

ANSWER ❶ You don't need to dress up for the party. ❷ On 'no-tie' days, people take off their ties and dress down. ❸ You can count me in for the dinner! ❹ Thanks for the invitation, but count me out this time. I am too busy at the moment. ❺ Hurry, Sara is waiting in line for us at the restaurant. ❻ Cutting in line is bad manners. ❼ The subway is connected to the HS building. You won't miss it. ❽ Make sure you disconnect the cable before removing the component.

반대가 끌리는 이유, 짝꿍 동사들

반대의 뜻을 가진 짝꿍 동사 표현들로 이루어진 실제 대화에 도전!
음원을 들으며 영어문장을 따라 말해보세요.

음원 듣기

Ⓐ Can we meet so we can resolve the misunderstanding between us?

Ⓑ I misunderstood you?

Ⓐ Please, let's meet and talk.

Ⓑ We were waiting in line in front of the pasta restaurant and a couple cut in line in front of us.

Ⓐ I know they were wrong. But I didn't want to argue with the couple.

Ⓑ I've been stressed out from work and it felt like there was nobody on my side.

Ⓐ 만나서 우리 사이에 오해를 좀 풀자.

Ⓑ 내가 너를 오해했다고?

Ⓐ 제발. 만나서 얘기해.

Ⓑ 우리가 파스타 집 앞에서 줄 서서 기다리고 있는 중이었고, 한 커플이 새치기한 거 잖아.

Ⓐ 나도 그들이 잘못했다는 거 알아. 하지만 그 사람들과 다투고 싶지 않았어.

Ⓑ 요즘 직장에서 스트레스도 받는데, 내 편은 아무도 없는 것 같았어.

기본동사별 필수표현

week 11

이것만 알아도 영어가 쉬워진다! 기본이 되는 핵심 동사들 1

day 51 기본동사 do

영어의 기본이 되는 핵심동사 do와 관련된 표현입니다.

음원을 듣고 영어표현을 따라 말한 후, 손으로 써보세요.

1st step ★ 따라 **말**하고 **써**보며 표현 **익**히기

음원 듣기

1. 무언가를 하다 ▶ do something/anything
2. 숙제를 하다 ▶ do one's homework
3. 다리미질을 하다 ▶ do some ironing
4. 청소를 하다 ▶ do the cleaning
5. 설거지를 하다 ▶ do the dishes
6. 푸시업/윗몸일으키기를 하다 ▶ do push-ups/sit-ups
7. 문서 작업들을 하다 ▶ do some paperwork
8. 최선을 다하다 ▶ do one's best on

앞에서 배운 표현을 떠올리며 한글에 해당하는 영어문장을 만들어보세요.

전체 문장을 만드는 게 어렵다면 오른쪽 옆 페이지를 참고하세요.

2nd step ★ 문장 속 표현 **확인**하기

❶ 나 주말 동안 아무것도 안 했어.

❷ 나는 수업 후에 바로 숙제를 해.

❸ 내일을 위해 다리미질을 해야 해.

❹ 누가 청소할 차례야?

❺ 먹자마자 설거지해.

❻ 나는 매일 푸시업과 윗몸일으키기를 100개씩 해.

❼ 그 워크샵을 위해 해야 할 문서 작업이 좀 있어.

❽ 나는 그 발표를 위해 최선을 다했어.

ANSWER ❶ I didn't do anything over the weekend. ❷ I do my homework right after class. ❸ I need to do some ironing for tomorrow. ❹ Whose turn is it to do the cleaning? ❺ Do the dishes right after you are done eating. ❻ I do 100 push-ups and sit-ups every day. ❼ I have some paperwork to do for the workshop. ❽ I did my best on the presentation.

빈칸에 해당하는 표현을 채우며 한 번 더 복습해보세요.

먼저 만든 전체 문장을 떠올리며 빈칸을 채워보세요.

3rd step ★ 한 번 **더 더블**체크!

❶ I didn't ______ ______ over the weekend.
→ 무언가를 하다
• 부정문에서는 anything 긍정문에서는 something

❷ I ______ ______ ______ right after class.
→ 숙제를 하다

❸ I need to ______ ______ ______ for tomorrow.
→ 다리미질을 하다

❹ Whose turn is it to ______ ______ ______ ?
→ 청소를 하다

❺ ______ ______ ______ right after you are done eating.
→ 설거지를 하다

❻ I ______ 100 ______ and sit-ups every day.
→ 푸시업을 하다

❼ I have ______ ______ to ______ for the workshop.
→ 문서 작업들을 하다

❽ I ______ ______ ______ ______ the presentation.
→ 최선을 다했다

ANSWER ❶ do anything ❷ do my homework ❸ do some ironing ❹ do the cleaning ❺ Do the dishes ❻ do, push-ups ❼ some paperwork, do ❽ did my best on

음원을 듣고 영어문장을 받아써보세요.

음원을 들으면서 원어민의 목소리를 성대모사하듯 입으로 소리내어 연습해보세요.

4th step ★ 최종점검! 영어문장 **받아써**보기 음원 듣기 

❶ HINT weekend

❷ HINT right

❸ HINT ironing

❹ HINT turn

❺ HINT done

❻ HINT push-ups, sit-ups

❼ HINT paperwork

❽ HINT presentation

ANSWER ❶ I didn't do anything over the weekend. ❷ I do my homework right after class. ❸ I need to do some ironing for tomorrow. ❹ Whose turn is it to do the cleaning? ❺ Do the dishes right after you are done eating. ❻ I do 100 push-ups and sit-ups every day. ❼ I have some paperwork to do for the workshop. ❽ I did my best on the presentation.

day 52 기본동사 get

영어의 기본이 되는 핵심동사
get과 관련된 표현입니다.

음원을 듣고 영어표현을 따라 말한 후, 손으로 써보세요.

1st step ★ 따라 **말**하고 **써**보며 표현 **익**히기

음원 듣기

❶ 이해하다 ▶ get the/one's point

❷ 휴식하다 ▶ get some rest

❸ 주사 맞다 ▶ get a shot

❹ 모이다 ▶ get together

❺ 극복하다 ▶ get over

❻ 점점 나아지다/나빠지다 ▶ get better/worse

❼ 나이 먹어가다, 늙어가다 ▶ get old(er)

❽ (근근이, 그럭저럭) 살다 ▶ get by

앞에서 배운 표현을 떠올리며 한글에 해당하는 영어문장을 만들어보세요.

전체 문장을 만드는 게 어렵다면 오른쪽 옆 페이지를 참고하세요.

2nd step ★ 문장 속 표현 **확인**하기

❶ 제 말 이해하시나요?

❷ 집에 가서 좀 쉬어.

❸ 나 주사 맞는 거 너무 무서워.

❹ 우리 언제 모여서 술 한잔 하는 거 어때요?

❺ 그 사람과 (헤어진 거) 극복하는 데 1주일도 안 걸리더라.

❻ 나 믿어봐. 상황이 좋아지고 있어.

❼ 나이 먹는 것을 멈출 수 없지만, 늙을 필요는 없지요.

❽ 나는 그럭저럭 살기에 충분한 돈을 가지고 있어.

ANSWER ❶ Do you get my point? ❷ Go home and get some rest. ❸ I am so scared of getting shots. ❹ How about we get together for a drink sometime? ❺ It took me less than a week to get over him. ❻ Trust me. Things are getting better. ❼ You can't help getting older, but you don't have to get old. ❽ I just have enough money to get by.

빈칸에 해당하는 표현을 채우며 한 번 더 복습해보세요.

먼저 만든 전체 문장을 떠올리며 빈칸을 채워보세요.

3rd step ★ 한 번 **더 더블**체크!

❶ Do you ______ my ______ ?
→ 이해하다

❷ Go home and ______ ______ ______ .
→ 휴식하다

❸ I am so scared of ______ ______ .
→ 주사 맞는 것

❹ How about we ______ ______ for a drink sometime?
→ 모이다

❺ It took me less than a week to ______ ______ him.
→ 극복하다

❻ Trust me. Things are ______ ______ .
→ 점점 나아지다 • –ing 현재진행형

❼ You can't help getting older, but you don't have to ______ ______ .
→ 늙어가다

❽ I just have enough money to ______ ______ .
→ (근근이, 그럭저럭) 살다

ANSWER ❶ get, point ❷ get some rest ❸ getting shots ❹ get together ❺ get over ❻ getting better ❼ get old ❽ get by

음원을 듣고 영어문장을 받아써보세요.

음원을 들으면서 원어민의 목소리를 성대모사하듯
입으로 소리내어 연습해보세요.

4th step ★ 최종점검! 영어문장 **받아써**보기 음원 듣기

❶ HINT point

❷ HINT rest

❸ HINT scared, shots

❹ HINT together

❺ HINT less, than

❻ HINT trust

❼ HINT can't, help

❽ HINT enough

ANSWER ❶ Do you get my point? ❷ Go home and get some rest. ❸ I am so scared of getting shots. ❹ How about we get together for a drink sometime? ❺ It took me less than a week to get over him. ❻ Trust me. Things are getting better. ❼ You can't help getting older, but you don't have to get old. ❽ I just have enough money to get by.

day 53 기본동사 give

영어의 기본이 되는 핵심동사
give와 관련된 표현입니다.

음원을 듣고 영어표현을 따라 말한 후, 손으로 써보세요.

1st step ★ 따라 **말**하고 **써**보며 표현 **익**히기

음원 듣기

❶ ~에게 돈/시간을 주다 ▶ give ~ money/time

❷ ~를 도와주다 ▶ give+사람+a hand/help

❸ ~에게 강연/발표를 하다 ▶ give ~ a lecture/presentation

❹ ~를 흘끗 보다 ▶ give+사람+a look

❺ 시도하다 ▶ give it a try

❻ ~를 태워다주다 ▶ give+사람+a ride

❼ ~에게 자신감을 주다 ▶ give+사람+confidence

❽ ~에게 안부를 전해주다 ▶ give one's regards to ~

앞에서 배운 표현을 떠올리며 한글에 해당하는 영어문장을 만들어보세요.

전체 문장을 만드는 게 어렵다면 오른쪽 옆 페이지를 참고하세요.

2nd step ★ 문장 속 표현 **확인**하기

❶ 미안하지만 나에게 시간을 좀 더 줄 수 있어?

❷ 내가 이 박스들 (나르는 거) 도와줄게.

❸ 그는 첫인상이 얼마나 중요한지에 대해서 강연을 할 거야.

❹ 그가 나를 이상하게 쳐다봤어.

❺ 그냥 한번 해봐. 잃을 게 뭐 있겠어.

❻ 내가 집에 데려다줄게.

❼ 저 막 30살이 되었어요. 제 나이는 제게 자신감을 줘요.

❽ 당신 부모님께 안부 전해주세요.

ANSWER ❶ I am sorry but could you give me some more time? ❷ I will give you a hand with those boxes. ❸ He will give a lecture on how important first impressions are. ❹ He gave me a strange look. ❺ Just give it a try. You have nothing to lose. ❻ I will give you a ride home. ❼ I just turned 30. My age gives me confidence. ❽ Give my regards to your parents.

빈칸에 해당하는 표현을 채우며 한 번 더 복습해보세요.

먼저 만든 전체 문장을 떠올리며 빈칸을 채워보세요.

3rd step ★ 한 번 **더 더블**체크!

❶ I am sorry but could you ______ ______ some more ______?
→ ~에게 시간을 주다

❷ I will ______ you ______ ______ with those boxes.
→ ~를 도와주다

❸ He will ______ ______ ______ on how important first impressions are.
→ ~에게 강연을 하다

❹ He ______ me ______ strange ______.
→ ~를 흘끗 보았다

❺ Just ______ ______ ______ ______. You have nothing to lose.
→ 시도하다

❻ I will ______ you ______ ______ home.
→ ~를 태워다주다

❼ I just turned 30. My age ______ me ______.
→ ~에게 자신감을 주다

❽ ______ ______ ______ ______ your parents.
→ ~에게 안부를 전해주다

ANSWER ❶ give me, time ❷ give, a hand ❸ give a lecture ❹ gave, a, look ❺ give it a try ❻ give, a ride ❼ gives, confidence ❽ Give my regards to

음원을 듣고 영어문장을 받아써보세요.

음원을 들으면서 원어민의 목소리를 성대모사하듯 입으로 소리내어 연습해보세요.

4th step ★ 최종점검! 영어문장 **받아써**보기

음원 듣기 

❶ HINT could

❷ HINT those, boxes

❸ HINT impressions

❹ HINT strange

❺ HINT lose

❻ HINT ride

❼ HINT turned, confidence

❽ HINT regards

ANSWER ❶ I am sorry but could you give me some more time? ❷ I will give you a hand with those boxes. ❸ He will give a lecture on how important first impressions are. ❹ He gave me a strange look. ❺ Just give it a try. You have nothing to lose. ❻ I will give you a ride home. ❼ I just turned 30. My age gives me confidence. ❽ Give my regards to your parents.

day 54 기본동사 have

영어의 기본이 되는 핵심동사 have와 관련된 표현입니다.

음원을 듣고 영어표현을 따라 말한 후, 손으로 써보세요.

1st step ★ 따라 **말**하고 **써**보며 표현 **익**히기

음원 듣기

❶ 돈/시간이 있다 ▸ have money/time

❷ 아침을 먹다/커피를 마시다 ▸ have breakfast/coffee

❸ 간식을 먹다 ▸ have a snack

❹ 쉬는 시간을 갖다 ▸ have a break

❺ 즐거운 시간을 갖다 ▸ have a good time/day

❻ 남은 시간을 즐겁게 보내다 ▸ have a good rest of the day/week

❼ 즐거운 여행을 하다 ▸ have a good trip

❽ (~하는 데) 문제가 있다 ▸ have a problem (-ing)

앞에서 배운 표현을 떠올리며 한글에 해당하는 영어문장을 만들어보세요.

전체 문장을 만드는 게 어렵다면 오른쪽 옆 페이지를 참고하세요.

2nd step ★ 문장 속 표현 **확인**하기

❶ 저는 시간이 많지 않아요.

❷ 언제 차 한잔 함께해요.

❸ 나는 식사 사이에 간식을 먹어.

❹ 나 3시에 쉬는 시간 있어.

❺ 오늘 밤 즐겁게 보내세요!

❻ 남은 하루 즐겁게 보내세요!

❼ 일본에서 즐거운 여행하세요.

❽ 나는 그 사람의 억양을 이해하기가 힘들어.

ANSWER ❶ I don't have much time. ❷ Let's have a cup of tea at some point later. ❸ I usually have a snack between meals. ❹ I have a break at 3 o'clock today. ❺ Have a good time tonight! ❻ Have a good rest of the day! ❼ Have a good trip in Japan. ❽ I have a problem understanding his accent.

빈칸에 해당하는 표현을 채우며 한 번 더 복습해보세요.

먼저 만든 전체 문장을 떠올리며 빈칸을 채워보세요.

3rd step ★ 한 번 **더 더블**체크!

❶ I don't ______ much ______ .
→ 시간이 있다

❷ Let's ______ a cup of ______ at some point later.
→ 차를 마시다

❸ I usually ______ ______ ______ between meals.
→ 간식을 먹다

❹ I ______ ______ ______ at 3 o'clock today.
→ 쉬는 시간을 갖다

❺ ______ ______ ______ ______ tonight!
→ 즐거운 시간을 갖다

❻ ______ ______ ______ ______ ______ ______ day!
→ 남은 시간을 즐겁게 보내다

❼ ______ ______ ______ ______ in Japan.
→ 즐거운 여행을 하다

❽ I ______ ______ ______ understanding his accent.
→ (~하는 데) 문제가 있다

ANSWER ❶ have, time ❷ have, tea ❸ have a snack ❹ have a break ❺ Have a good time ❻ Have a good rest of the ❼ Have a good trip ❽ have a problem

음원을 듣고 영어문장을 받아써보세요.

음원을 들으면서 원어민의 목소리를 성대모사하듯
입으로 소리내어 연습해보세요.

4th step ★ 최종점검! 영어문장 **받아써**보기 음원 듣기

❶ HINT much

❷ HINT point

❸ HINT meals

❹ HINT break

❺ HINT tonight

❻ HINT rest

❼ HINT trip, Japan

❽ HINT accent

ANSWER ❶ I don't have much time. ❷ Let's have a cup of tea at some point later. ❸ I usually have a snack between meals. ❹ I have a break at 3 o'clock today. ❺ Have a good time tonight! ❻ Have a good rest of the day! ❼ Have a good trip in Japan. ❽ I have a problem understanding his accent.

day 55 기본동사 keep

영어의 기본이 되는 핵심동사
keep과 관련된 표현입니다.

음원을 듣고 영어표현을 따라 말한 후, 손으로 써보세요.

1st step ★ 따라 **말**하고 **써**보며 표현 **익**히기

음원 듣기

❶ 비밀로 하다, 비밀을 유지하다 ▶ keep a secret

❷ 약속을 지키다 ▶ keep a promise

❸ 일기를 (꾸준히) 쓰다 ▶ keep a diary

❹ ~을 따뜻하게 유지하다 ▶ keep ~ warm

❺ 연락하고 지내다 ▶ keep in touch

❻ ~의 내용을 명심하다 ▶ keep ~ in mind

❼ ~의 기록을 관리하다 ▶ keep track of -ing

❽ ~을 계속 해나가다, 계속 파이팅하다 ▶ keep up ~

앞에서 배운 표현을 떠올리며 한글에 해당하는 영어문장을 만들어보세요.

전체 문장을 만드는 게 어렵다면 오른쪽 옆 페이지를 참고하세요.

2nd step ★ 문장 속 표현 **확인**하기

❶ 너 비밀 지킬 수 있어?

❷ 네가 한 약속을 지키는 건 중요해.

❸ 일기 쓰세요?

❹ 겨울에는 방을 꼭 따뜻하게 유지하세요.

❺ 고등학교 친구들과 연락하고 지내니?

❻ 나 그거 마음에 새기고, 같은 실수 다신 안 할 거야.

❼ 지출 기록을 관리하세요?

❽ 지금처럼만 해! (잘 하고 있어!)

ANSWER ❶ Can you keep a secret? ❷ Keeping your promises is important ❸ Do you keep a diary? ❹ Make sure you keep your room warm during winter. ❺ Do you keep in touch with your high school friends? ❻ I'll keep that in mind, so I don't make the same mistake again. ❼ Do you keep track of your spending? ❽ Keep up the good work!

빈칸에 해당하는 표현을 채우며 한 번 더 복습해보세요.

먼저 만든 전체 문장을 떠올리며 빈칸을 채워보세요.

3rd step ★ 한 번 **더 더블**체크!

❶ Can you ______ ______ ______ ?

→ 비밀로 하다

❷ ______ your ______ is important.

→ 약속을 지키는 것

❸ Do you ______ ______ ______ ?

→ 일기를 (꾸준히) 쓰다

❹ Make sure you ______ your room ______ during winter.

→ ~을 따뜻하게 유지하다

❺ Do you ______ ______ ______ with your high school friends?

→ 연락을 하고 지내다

❻ I'll ______ that ______ ______ , so I don't make the same mistake again.

→ ~의 내용을 명심하다

❼ Do you ______ ______ ______ your spending?

→ ~의 기록을 관리하다

❽ ______ ______ the good work!

→ ~을 계속 해나가다, 계속 파이팅하다

ANSWER ❶ keep a secret ❷ Keeping, promises ❸ keep a diary ❹ keep, warm ❺ keep in touch ❻ keep, in mind ❼ keep track of ❽ Keep up

음원을 듣고 영어문장을 받아써보세요.

음원을 들으면서 원어민의 목소리를 성대모사하듯 입으로 소리내어 연습해보세요.

4th step ★ 최종점검! 영어문장 **받아써**보기

음원 듣기 

❶ HINT secret

❷ HINT promise

❸ HINT diary

❹ HINT warm

❺ HINT touch

❻ HINT mistake

❼ HINT spending

❽ HINT work

ANSWER ❶ Can you keep a secret? ❷ Keeping your promises is important. ❸ Do you keep a diary? ❹ Make sure you keep your room warm during winter. ❺ Do you keep in touch with your high school friends? ❻ I'll keep that in mind, so I don't make the same mistake again. ❼ Do you keep track of your spending? ❽ Keep up the good work!

기본이 되는 핵심 동사들 1

영어의 기본동사 표현들로 이루어진 실제 대화에 도전!
음원을 들으며 영어문장을 따라 말해보세요.

음원 듣기

A I have to give a presentation on our new products. I can't speak while looking into other people's eyes.

B You can give it a try. I'm doing some paperwork right now but I can give you some tips later.

> Lunch Break

A You have to tell me how I can get over my fear.

B Memorize your key points and record yourself on camera. Keep that in mind!

A I get the point, but it will be really awkward to watch myself on video.

B I was really bad at presenting in the past, but I fixed it by recording myself.

A 우리 새 제품에 대해 프레젠테이션을 해야 하는데. 사람들 눈 쳐다보면서 말하는 거 못하겠어.

B 그냥 한번 시도해봐. 나 지금 문서작업 중인데, 이따가 팁을 좀 줄 수 있어.

> 점심 시간

A 어떻게 두려움을 극복할 수 있을지 나한테 말해줘야 해.

B 요점을 암기하고, 네 모습을 카메라로 녹화하도록 해. 명심해!

A 알겠어. 그런데 내 모습을 비디오로 보는 건 정말 어색할 거야.

B 나도 전에는 프레젠테이션 정말 못했었는데, 내 모습을 녹화하면서 고쳤어.

week 12

이것만 알아도 영어가 쉬워진다!
기본이 되는 핵심 동사들 2

day 56 기본동사 make

day 57 기본동사 take

day 58 기본동사 go

day 59 기본동사 miss

day 60 기본동사 lose

day 56 기본동사 make

영어의 기본이 되는 핵심동사 make와 관련된 표현입니다.

음원을 듣고 영어표현을 따라 말한 후, 손으로 써보세요.

1st step ★ 따라 **말**하고 **써**보며 표현 **익**히기

음원 듣기

❶ 노력하다 ▸ make an effort

❷ 분란을 일으키다 ▸ make a trouble

❸ 실수하다 ▸ make a mistake

❹ 결심하다, 결정하다 ▸ make a decision

❺ 변명하다 ▸ make an excuse

❻ 바꾸다, 변화를 만들다 ▸ make a change/difference

❼ 성공하다 ▸ make it

❽ (~에) 진전을 보이다 ▸ make progress (on ~)

앞에서 배운 표현을 떠올리며 한글에 해당하는 영어문장을 만들어보세요.

전체 문장을 만드는 게 어렵다면 오른쪽 옆 페이지를 참고하세요.

2nd step ★ 문장 속 표현 **확인**하기

❶ 나는 면접관들에 좋은 인상을 주기 위해 노력했어.

❷ 분란을 일으키고 싶지 않지만, 이제 변화를 줄 때야.

❸ 내가 한 가장 큰 실수는 학교를 끝마치지 못한 거야.

❹ 우리 지금 바로 결정해야 해.

❺ 왜 늦었어? 변명하지 말고.

❻ 내년에는 어떤 변화를 만들고 싶어? (어떻게 변하고 싶어?)

❼ 너는 해낼 거야. 그냥 계속 시도해.

❽ 우리는 트레이닝 프로그램에 도약이 필요해요.

ANSWER ❶ I made an effort to impress the interviewers. ❷ I don't want to make any trouble but it's time for a change. ❸ The biggest mistake I made was not completing my education. ❹ We need to make a decision right now. ❺ Why are you late? Don't make any excuses. ❻ What changes do you want to make next year? ❼ You will make it. Just keep trying. ❽ We need to make progress with the training program.

빈칸에 해당하는 표현을 채우며 한 번 더 복습해보세요.

먼저 만든 전체 문장을 떠올리며 빈칸을 채워보세요.

3rd step ★ 한 번 **더 더블**체크!

❶ I ______ ______ ______ to impress the interviewers.
→ 노력했다

❷ I don't want to ______ any ______ but it's time for a change.
→ 분란을 일으키다

❸ The biggest ______ I ______ was not completing my education.
→ 실수했다

❹ We need to ______ ______ ______ right now.
→ 결심하다, 결정하다

❺ Why are you late? Don't ______ any ______.
→ 변명하다

❻ What ______ do you want to ______ next year?
→ 바꾸다, 변화를 만들다

❼ You will ______ ______. Just keep trying.
→ 성공하다

❽ We need to ______ ______ with the training program.
→ (~에) 진전을 보이다

ANSWER ❶ made an effort ❷ make, trouble ❸ mistake, made ❹ make a decision ❺ make, excuses ❻ changes, make ❼ make it ❽ make progress

음원을 듣고 영어문장을 받아써보세요.

음원을 들으면서 원어민의 목소리를 성대모사하듯 입으로 소리내어 연습해보세요.

4th step ★ 최종점검! 영어문장 **받아써**보기

음원 듣기 

❶ HINT interviewers

❷ HINT trouble

❸ HINT completing

❹ HINT decision

❺ HINT excuses

❻ HINT changes

❼ HINT trying

❽ HINT progress

ANSWER ❶ I made an effort to impress the interviewers. ❷ I don't want to make any trouble but it's time for a change. ❸ The biggest mistake I made was not completing my education. ❹ We need to make a decision right now. ❺ Why are you late? Don't make any excuses. ❻ What changes do you want to make next year? ❼ You will make it. Just keep trying. ❽ We need to make progress with the training program.

day 57 기본동사 take

영어의 기본이 되는 핵심동사 take와 관련된 표현입니다.

음원을 듣고 영어표현을 따라 말한 후, 손으로 써보세요.

1st step ★ 따라 **말**하고 **써**보며 표현 **익**히기

음원 듣기

❶ ~를 집에 데려다주다 ▸ take+사람+home

❷ ~를 …로 데려다주다 ▸ take+사람+to+장소

❸ 수업/코스를 듣다 ▸ take a class/course

❹ 시험을 보다 ▸ take a test, take an exam

❺ ~의 사진을 찍다 ▸ take a picture of ~

❻ 위험을 감수하다 ▸ take risks

❼ 시간이 걸리다 ▸ It takes time

❽ ~하는 데 …의 시간이 걸리다 ▸ It takes ... hours to ~

앞에서 배운 표현을 떠올리며 한글에 해당하는 영어문장을 만들어보세요.

전체 문장을 만드는 게 어렵다면 오른쪽 옆 페이지를 참고하세요.

2nd step ★ 문장 속 표현 **확인**하기

❶ 게일이 너를 집에 데려다줄 거야.

❷ 아들이 아파서 병원에 데려가야 해요.

❸ 이번 학기에 수업 몇 개 들어?

❹ IQ 테스트 본 적 있어?

❺ 우리 사진 좀 찍어주시겠어요?

❻ 기업가들은 위험을 감수할 준비가 되어 있어야 해.

❼ 시간이 좀 걸릴 거야.

❽ 학교 가는 데 1시간 정도 걸려요.

ANSWER ❶ Gayle will take you home. ❷ My son is sick so I have to take him to the hospital. ❸ How many classes are you taking this semester? ❹ Have you taken an IQ test? ❺ Could you take a picture of us? ❻ Entrepreneurs should be prepared to take risks. ❼ It will take some time. ❽ It takes about 1 hour to get to school.

빈칸에 해당하는 표현을 채우며 한 번 더 복습해보세요.

먼저 만든 전체 문장을 떠올리며 빈칸을 채워보세요.

3rd step ★ 한 번 **더 더블**체크!

❶ Gayle will ______ you ______.
→ ~를 집에 데려다주다

❷ My son is sick so I have to ______ him ______ the hospital.
→ ~를 …로 데려다주다

❸ How many ______ are you ______ this semester?
→ 수업을 듣고 있다

❹ Have you ______ ______ IQ ______?
→ 시험을 보았다

❺ Could you ______ ______ ______ ______ us?
→ ~의 사진을 찍다

❻ Entrepreneurs should be prepared to ______ ______.
→ 위험을 감수하다

❼ ______ will ______ some ______.
→ 시간이 걸리다

❽ ______ ______ about 1 ______ ______ get to school.
→ ~하는 데 …의 시간이 걸리다

ANSWER ❶ take, home ❷ take, to ❸ classes, taking ❹ taken an, test ❺ take a picture of ❻ take risks ❼ It, take, time ❽ It takes, hour to

음원을 듣고 영어문장을 받아써보세요.

음원을 들으면서 원어민의 목소리를 성대모사하듯 입으로 소리내어 연습해보세요.

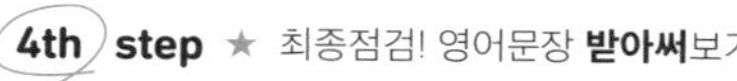

4th step ★ 최종점검! 영어문장 **받아써**보기

음원 듣기 

❶ HINT take

❷ HINT son, hospital

❸ HINT semester

❹ HINT IQ test

❺ HINT picture

❻ HINT Entrepreneurs

❼ HINT will

❽ HINT hour

ANSWER ❶ Gayle will take you home. ❷ My son is sick so I have to take him to the hospital. ❸ How many classes are you taking this semester? ❹ Have you taken an IQ test? ❺ Could you take a picture of us? ❻ Entrepreneurs should be prepared to take risks. ❼ It will take some time. ❽ It takes about 1 hour to get to school.

day 58 기본동사 go

영어의 기본이 되는 핵심동사
go와 관련된 표현입니다.

음원을 듣고 영어표현을 따라 말한 후, 손으로 써보세요.

1st step ★ 따라 **말**하고 **써**보며 표현 **익**히기

음원 듣기

❶ 휴가를 가다 ▸ go on a vacation

❷ 산책/드라이브를 가다 ▸ go for a walk/drive

❸ 식사하러/술 마시러 가다 ▸ go for a meal/drink

❹ 등산가다 ▸ go hiking

❺ 낚시하러 가다 ▸ go fishing

❻ 관광 가다 ▸ go sightseeing

❼ 병원에 가다 ▸ go see a doctor

❽ 치과에 가다 ▸ go see a dentist

앞에서 배운 표현을 떠올리며 한글에 해당하는 영어문장을 만들어보세요.

전체 문장을 만드는 게 어렵다면 오른쪽 옆 페이지를 참고하세요.

2nd step ★ 문장 속 표현 **확인**하기

❶ 가능하다면 휴가 가고 싶어.

❷ 우리 영화 대신에 드라이브 가는 거 어때요?

❸ 모여서 술 한잔하러 갑시다!

❹ 정말로 나랑 등산 가고 싶어?

❺ 우리 남편은 낚시 가는 거 좋아해요.

❻ 저는 이국적인 장소들 관광하는 거 좋아해요.

❼ 몸이 안 좋아. 나 병원에 가봐야 할 것 같아.

❽ 나 치통이 있어. 치과 가야겠어.

ANSWER ❶ I would like to go on a vacation, if possible. ❷ How about we go for a drive instead of the cinema? ❸ Let's get together and go for a drink! ❹ Do you really want to go hiking with me? ❺ My husband likes to go fishing. ❻ I like going sightseeing in exotic places. ❼ I don't feel well. I think I should go see a doctor. ❽ I have a toothache. I need to go see a dentist.

빈칸에 해당하는 표현을 채우며 한 번 더 복습해보세요.

먼저 만든 전체 문장을 떠올리며 빈칸을 채워보세요.

3rd step ★ 한 번 **더 더블**체크!

❶ I would like to ＿＿＿＿＿＿＿＿＿＿＿＿, if possible.
→ 휴가를 가다

❷ How about we ＿＿＿＿＿＿＿＿＿＿ instead of the cinema?
→ 드라이브를 가다

❸ Let's get together and ＿＿＿＿＿＿＿＿＿＿＿＿!
→ 술 마시러 가다

❹ Do you really want to ＿＿＿＿＿＿ with me?
→ 등산 가다

❺ My husband likes to ＿＿＿＿＿＿.
→ 낚시하러 가다

❻ I like ＿＿＿＿＿＿ in exotic places.
→ 관광 가는 것

❼ I don't feel well. I think I should ＿＿＿＿＿＿＿＿＿＿＿＿.
→ 병원에 가다

❽ I have a toothache. I need to ＿＿＿＿＿＿＿＿＿＿＿＿.
→ 치과에 가다

ANSWER ❶ go on a vacation ❷ go for a drive ❸ go for a drink ❹ go hiking ❺ go fishing ❻ going sightseeing ❼ go see a doctor ❽ go see a dentist

day 58

음원을 듣고 영어문장을 받아써보세요.

음원을 들으면서 원어민의 목소리를 성대모사하듯
입으로 소리내어 연습해보세요.

4th step ★ 최종점검! 영어문장 **받아써**보기

음원 듣기 

❶ HINT vacation

❷ HINT instead, cinema

❸ HINT drink

❹ HINT hiking

❺ HINT husband

❻ HINT exotic

❼ HINT feel, well

❽ HINT toothache, dentist

ANSWER ❶ I would like to go on a vacation, if possible. ❷ How about we go for a drive instead of the cinema? ❸ Let's get together and go for a drink! ❹ Do you really want to go hiking with me? ❺ My husband likes to go fishing. ❻ I like going sightseeing in exotic places. ❼ I don't feel well. I think I should go see a doctor. ❽ I have a toothache. I need to go see a dentist.

day 59 기본동사 miss

영어의 기본이 되는 핵심동사 miss와 관련된 표현입니다.

음원을 듣고 영어표현을 따라 말한 후, 손으로 써보세요.

1st step ★ 따라 **말**하고 **써**보며 표현 **익**히기

음원 듣기

❶ ~를 그리워하다 ▸ miss+사람

❷ ~했던 시간을 그리워하다 ▸ miss the time ~

❸ 버스를 놓치다 ▸ miss the bus

❹ 수업을 놓치다/빠지다 ▸ miss the class

❺ 기회를 놓치다 ▸ miss the chance

❻ (숙어) 기회를 놓치다 ▸ miss the boat

❼ 요점을 놓치다 ▸ miss the/one's point

❽ (예약해둔) 약속에 가지 못하다 ▸ miss the appointment

앞에서 배운 표현을 떠올리며 한글에 해당하는 영어문장을 만들어보세요.

전체 문장을 만드는 게 어렵다면 오른쪽 옆 페이지를 참고하세요.

2nd step ★ 문장 속 표현 **확인**하기

❶ 나는 아직 전 남자친구를 그리워하는 것 같아.

❷ 나는 우리가 함께 보냈던 시간이 그리워.

❸ 천만다행이다! 버스를 거의 놓칠 뻔 했어.

❹ 수업을 빠지게 되면 어쩌지?

❺ 승진할 기회를 놓치고 싶지 않아.

❻ 그 브랜드 지난주에는 세일이었는데, 기회를 놓쳤어.

❼ 너 내 요점을 놓치고 있는 것 같아. 다시 설명해볼게.

❽ 병원 예약을 못 갔어.

ANSWER ❶ I think I still miss my ex-boyfriend. ❷ I miss the time we spent together. ❸ Thank goodness! I almost missed the bus. ❹ What do I do if I miss the class? ❺ I don't want to miss the chance to get a promotion. ❻ The brand was on sale last week but I missed the boat. ❼ I think you are missing my point. Let me explain it again. ❽ I had to miss the doctor's appointment.

빈칸에 해당하는 표현을 채우며 한 번 더 복습해보세요.

먼저 만든 전체 문장을 떠올리며 빈칸을 채워보세요.

3rd step ★ 한 번 **더 더블**체크!

❶ I think I still ________ my ex-boyfriend.
→ ~를 그리워하다

❷ I ________ ________ ________ we spent together.
→ ~했던 시간을 그리워하다

❸ Thank goodness! I almost ________ ________ ________.
→ 버스를 놓쳤다

❹ What do I do if I ________ ________ ________?
→ 수업을 놓치다

❺ I don't want to ________ ________ ________ to get a promotion.
→ 기회를 놓치다

❻ The brand was on sale last week but I ________ ________ ________.
→ 기회를 놓쳤다

❼ I think you are ________ ________ ________. Let me explain it again.
→ 요점을 놓치고 있다

❽ I had to ________ ________ doctor's ________.
→ (예약해둔) 약속에 가지 못하다

ANSWER ❶ miss ❷ miss the time ❸ missed the bus ❹ miss the class ❺ miss the chance ❻ missed the boat ❼ missing my point ❽ miss the, appointment

음원을 듣고 영어문장을 받아써보세요.

음원을 들으면서 원어민의 목소리를 성대모사하듯 입으로 소리내어 연습해보세요.

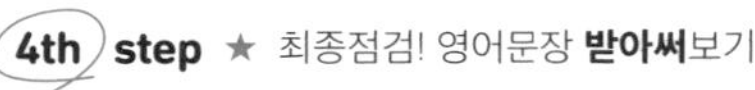
4th step ★ 최종점검! 영어문장 **받아써**보기

음원 듣기 

❶ HINT ex-boyfriend

❷ HINT spent

❸ HINT goodness

❹ HINT class

❺ HINT promotion

❻ HINT boat

❼ HINT explain

❽ HINT appointment

ANSWER ❶ I think I still miss my ex-boyfriend. ❷ I miss the time we spent together. ❸ Thank goodness! I almost missed the bus. ❹ What do I do if I miss the class? ❺ I don't want to miss the chance to get a promotion. ❻ The brand was on sale last week but I missed the boat. ❼ I think you are missing my point. Let me explain it again. ❽ I had to miss the doctor's appointment.

day 60 기본동사 lose

영어의 기본이 되는 핵심동사
lose와 관련된 표현입니다.

음원을 듣고 영어표현을 따라 말한 후, 손으로 써보세요.

1st step ★ 따라 **말**하고 **써**보며 표현 **익**히기

음원 듣기

❶ 우산을 잃어버리다 ▸ lose one's umbrella

❷ 게임에서 지다 ▸ lose the game

❸ (감기 등으로) 목소리를 잃다 ▸ lose one's voice

❹ ~에 흥미를 잃다 ▸ lose interest in ~

❺ 자신감을 잃다 ▸ lose one's confidence

❻ 균형을 잃다 ▸ lose one's balance

❼ 살을 빼다 ▸ lose weight

❽ ~하느라 시간 가는 줄 모르다 ▸ lose track of time (-ing)

앞에서 배운 표현을 떠올리며 한글에 해당하는 영어문장을 만들어보세요.

전체 문장을 만드는 게 어렵다면 오른쪽 옆 페이지를 참고하세요.

2nd step ★ 문장 속 표현 **확인**하기

❶ 우산을 또 잃어버린 거야? 참 부주의하다!

❷ 한국이 일본에 지다니 믿을 수가 없어.

❸ 목이 아프더니 다음날 목소리가 안 나왔어요.

❹ 나 나가서 친구들을 만나는 데 흥미를 잃었어.

❺ 나 자신감을 잃은 것 같아. 어떻게 되돌릴 수 있을까?

❻ 행복의 열쇠는 일과 삶의 균형을 잃지 않는 것이죠.

❼ 우리 건강한 방식으로 살을 빼야 해.

❽ 나는 축구할 때는, 시간 가는 줄 모르겠어.

ANSWER ❶ Did you lose your umbrella, again? So careless! ❷ I can't believe Korea lost the game against Japan. ❸ I had a sore throat so I lost my voice the next day. ❹ I have lost interest in going out and meeting friends. ❺ I think I lost my confidence. How can I get it back? ❻ The key to happiness is not to lose your work-life balance. ❼ We need to lose weight in a healthy way. ❽ When I play soccer, I lose track of time.

빈칸에 해당하는 표현을 채우며 한 번 더 복습해보세요.

먼저 만든 전체 문장을 떠올리며 빈칸을 채워보세요.

3rd step ★ 한 번 **더 더블**체크!

❶ Did you ______________ , again? So careless!
→ 우산을 잃어버리다

❷ I can't believe Korea ______________ against Japan.
→ 게임에서 졌다

❸ I had a sore throat so I ______________ the next day.
→ 목소리를 잃었다

❹ I have ______________ going out and meeting friends.
→ ~에 흥미를 잃었다

❺ I think I ______________ . How can I get it back?
→ 자신감을 잃었다

❻ The key to happiness is not to ______________ work-life ______________ .
→ 균형을 잃다

❼ We need to ______________ in a healthy way.
→ 살을 빼다

❽ When I play soccer, I ______________ .
→ ~하느라 시간 가는 줄 모르다

ANSWER ❶ lose your umbrella ❷ lost the game ❸ lost my voice ❹ lost interest in ❺ lost my confidence ❻ lose your, balance ❼ lose weight ❽ lose track of time

음원을 듣고 영어문장을 받아써보세요.

음원을 들으면서 원어민의 목소리를 성대모사하듯
입으로 소리내어 연습해보세요.

4th step ★ 최종점검! 영어문장 **받아써**보기

음원 듣기 

❶ HINT umbrella

❷ HINT against

❸ HINT sore, throat

❹ HINT going, out

❺ HINT confidence

❻ HINT work-life

❼ HINT way

❽ HINT soccer

ANSWER ❶ Did you lose your umbrella, again? So careless! ❷ I can't believe Korea lost the game against Japan. ❸ I had a sore throat so I lost my voice the next day. ❹ I have lost interest in going out and meeting friends. ❺ I think I lost my confidence. How can I get it back? ❻ The key to happiness is not to lose your work-life balance. ❼ We need to lose weight in a healthy way. ❽ When I play soccer, I lose track of time.

기본이 되는 핵심 동사들 2

영어의 기본동사 표현들로 이루어진 실제 대화에 도전!
음원을 들으며 영어문장을 따라 말해보세요.

음원 듣기

Ⓐ I used to lose track of time while working here, but I think I am losing interest in it.

Ⓑ Yes. You have been too busy working on the project. The key to happiness is to maintain your work-life balance.

Ⓐ You're right. I worked hard because I didn't want to miss any chances at work.

Ⓑ How about you take some time off and go on a trip or something? It will help you a lot.

Ⓐ I agree! Why don't we go for dinner tonight?

Ⓑ Sounds great!

Ⓐ 예전에는 여기서 일하느라 시간 가는 줄을 몰랐는데, 이제는 흥미를 좀 잃은 것 같아.

Ⓑ 맞아. 너 그 프로젝트 작업하느라 계속 너무 바빴잖아. 행복의 열쇠는 일과 삶의 균형을 잡는 거지.

Ⓐ 맞아. 직장에서 어떤 기회도 놓치고 싶지 않아서 열심히 일했어.

Ⓑ 휴가 내고 여행을 가보던가 하는 건 어때? 도움이 많이 될 거야.

Ⓐ 네 말이 맞아! 우리 오늘 함께 저녁 먹으러 가는 거 어때?

Ⓑ 좋아!

도전! 주제별 1분 스피치

맞벌이 부부의 한 주

앞에서 배운 표현을 활용한 주제별 스피치에 도전!
음원을 들으며 영어문장을 따라 말해보세요.

음원 듣기

We usually have a light breakfast and leave our place early because we don't like standing on crowded subways. After work, we get home around 8 pm. And we go to bed at around 11 at night. However, we stay up late on Fridays. These days, we watch a movie and enjoy a late night snack. On Saturdays, we sleep in and we catch up on house chores together. On Sundays, we play tennis together.

우리는 주로 간단하게 아침을 먹고 집을 일찍 나서요. 붐비는 지하철에서 서서 가고 싶지 않아서요. 일이 끝나면, 우리는 저녁 8시쯤 집에 도착합니다. 그리고 밤 11시쯤에 잠자리에 들어요. 하지만, 우리는 금요일에는 늦게 자요. 요즘 우리는 영화를 한 편 보고 치킨 같은 야식을 즐겨요. 토요일에는 늦게까지 잠을 자고 밀린 집안일을 함께하고요. 일요일에는 함께 테니스를 쳐요.

안정적인 일 vs. 좋아하는 일

앞에서 배운 표현을 활용한 주제별 스피치에 도전!
음원을 들으며 영어문장을 따라 말해보세요.

음원 듣기

My father used to work for the government. He thought it was important to have a stable job. But I don't think so. I am working for a travel agency. And people say this job isn't stable. But I am so happy with this job. I go on business trips abroad almost every month. I meet a lot of people from other countries and share ideas. I am happy even when I have to work on the weekend because I love this job.

제 아버지는 공무원으로 일하셨습니다. 아버지는 안정적인 직업을 가지는 것이 중요하다고 생각하셨죠. 하지만 저는 그렇게 생각하지 않아요. 저는 지금 한 여행사에서 근무하고 있어요. 그리고 사람들은 이 일이 안정적이지 않다고 말하죠. 하지만 저는 이 일에 만족해요. 저는 거의 매달 해외로 출장을 가요. 다른 나라에서 온 많은 사람들을 만나고 생각들을 공유해요. 저는 심지어 주말에 일해야 할 때도 행복해요. 제가 이 일을 사랑하니까요.

창업을 하려면

앞에서 배운 표현을 활용한 주제별 스피치에 도전!
음원을 들으며 영어문장을 따라 말해보세요.

음원 듣기

I was thinking of starting my own business so I met Sarah. Sarah is my friend and a successful business woman. She told me about how much effort she had put in for the past 3 years. She got up at 5 every day and read over 50 books to learn about managing a business. She met new people to learn business know-hows and kept up with cafe trends. After I heard her story, I was very motivated. I am living a busy life working and preparing for my new business. I am so happy and excited because I am working towards my dream.

나는 내 사업을 시작해볼 생각이 있어서 사라를 만났다. 사라는 내 친구이고, 성공한 비즈니스 사업가다. 그녀는 나에게 지난 3년 동안 그녀가 얼마나 많은 노력을 했는지에 대해서 말해주었다. 그녀는 매일 새벽 5시에 일어나서 사업을 운영하는 것에 대해 50권 이상의 책을 읽었다고 했다. 그녀는 사업 노하우를 배우고, 카페 트렌드를 읽기 위해서 새로운 사람들을 만났다. 그녀의 이야기를 들은 후에, 나는 동기부여가 많이 되었다. 지금 나는 일을 하고 새로운 사업도 준비하느라 바쁜 삶을 살고 있다. 나는 내 꿈을 향해 나아갈 수 있어서 너무 흥분되고 행복하다.

냉면의 깊은 맛

앞에서 배운 표현을 활용한 주제별 스피치에 도전!
음원을 들으며 영어문장을 따라 말해보세요.

음원 듣기

Last weekend, I lost my appetite due to the crazy hot weather. Nara said Pyeongyang cold noodles are the best to regain appetite so we went there. People were waiting in line at the restaurant. After we waited for about 30 minutes, we could finally taste the noodles. Actually when I took a sip of it, it tasted like nothing to me. The soup tasted under-seasoned. But after three or four more mouthfuls, I realized it had an interesting aftertaste. I think the place is worth waiting in line for!

지난 주말 날씨가 너무 더워서 나는 입맛을 잃어버렸다. 나라가 평양 냉면이 입맛을 돋우는 데는 최고라고 말해서 우리는 거기에 갔다. 사람들이 음식점에 줄을 서서 기다리고 있었다. 30분 정도 기다린 후에, 마침내 우리는 그 면을 맛볼 수 있었다. 사실 처음 한 입을 먹었을 때는, 아무 맛이 나지 않았다. 국물은 간이 덜 된 것 같았다. 하지만 세네 번 먹고 난 후, 나는 이 음식이 흥미로운 끝맛이 있다는 것을 알게 되었다. 나는 그곳이 기다릴 만한 가치가 있는 곳이라고 생각한다!

여행가방은 가볍게!

앞에서 배운 표현을 활용한 주제별 스피치에 도전!
음원을 들으며 영어문장을 따라 말해보세요.

음원 듣기

I have bad memories about packing for travel. Last year, my bag exceeded the weight limit so I had to pay extra for my overweight bag. And what's worse was, getting through customs took over 30 minutes because something sharp was somewhere in my bag. So I almost missed my flight. I felt like I had already ruined my trip. After that experience, I tend to pack lightly. I focus on enjoying the local scenery and on the last day, I buy some souvenirs. I get so excited because I can fill my empty luggage with new items.

나는 여행 짐 싸는 것에 대한 안 좋은 기억이 있다. 지난해, 내 가방이 무게 제한을 초과해서, 무게 초과 가방에 대해 추가 요금을 내야 했었다. 설상가상으로, 내 가방 속 어딘가에 뾰족한 물건 하나가 들어 있어, 세관을 통과하는 데에도 30분이 넘게 걸렸다. 그래서 비행기를 거의 놓칠 뻔 했다. 이미 여행을 망친 느낌이 들었다. 그 경험 후에, 나는 짐을 가볍게 싸는 경향이 있다. 나는 현지 경치를 즐기는 것에 집중하고, 마지막 날에 기념품들을 산다. 왜냐하면 빈 가방을 새로운 물건으로 채울 수 있어서, 정말 신이 나기 때문이다.

고등학교 친구들과의 여행

앞에서 배운 표현을 활용한 주제별 스피치에 도전!
음원을 들으며 영어문장을 따라 말해보세요.

음원 듣기

I went on a day trip to Gapyung with my high school friends last week. It was the first time meeting up after we all finished our military service. Sometimes I miss the time we spent together. We used to go to the same cram school and study together. We used to have a lot of fun back in our school days. I lost track of time talking with my friends during the night. We made a promise to go on an overseas trip together next summer.

저는 지난주에 고등학교 친구들과 가평으로 당일치기 여행을 갔어요. 우리 모두가 군대를 제대한 후로는 처음이었죠. 저는 가끔 우리가 함께했던 시간이 그리웠어요. 우리는 같은 입시학원에 다니면서 함께 공부를 했었어요. 학창시절을 돌아보면 정말 재미있었어요. 그날 밤 저는 친구들과 대화하며 시간 가는 줄 몰랐어요. 우리는 내년 여름에는 해외여행을 가기로 약속했어요.

부부의 새해 다짐

앞에서 배운 표현을 활용한 주제별 스피치에 도전!
음원을 들으며 영어문장을 따라 말해보세요.

음원 듣기

We made our new year's resolution. I am going to stop overspending. 2 weeks ago, we hired a financial advisor. He kept track of my spending and said I bought impulsively through online shopping sites. He was right. I buy lots of stuff and I don't use most of it. I should fix this bad habit. My husband decided to lose weight. He eats and drinks too much. He has gained over 5 kilos after getting married. He used to be of average build but now he is overweight. He's decided to exercise after work.

우리는 새해 결심을 만들었다. 나는 과소비하는 것을 끊기로 결심했다. 2주 전에, 우리는 재정 자문가 한 명을 고용했다. 그는 우리의 지출을 추적해보고 내가 온라인 쇼핑몰에서 충동구매를 많이 했다고 말했다. 그의 말이 맞았다. 나는 많은 물건을 사지만 그것들 중 대부분을 사용하지 않는다. 이 나쁜 습관을 고쳐야 한다. 남편은 살을 빼기로 결심했다. 그는 너무 많이 먹고 마신다. 결혼 후에 5kg이 넘게 살이 쪘다. 평균 체격이었는데 지금은 과체중이다. 그는 퇴근 후에 운동을 하기로 결심했다.

건강 관리는 필수

앞에서 배운 표현을 활용한 주제별 스피치에 도전!
음원을 들으며 영어문장을 따라 말해보세요.

음원 듣기

I get regular medical checkups every 2 years. The health test asked me about many things. I said I was taking nutrition supplements. And I often feel dizzy and I have a stiff neck. My doctor said the symptoms are signs of work-related stress. When she said stress can either be mentally and physically harmful, I recalled Minsoo because he was hospitalized due to stress from work before. I think I should make an effort to stay healthy and maintain my work-life balance.

나는 2년마다 건강 검진을 받는다. 건강 테스트는 나에게 많은 것들을 질문했다. 나는 영양 보조제 몇 개를 섭취하고 있다고 말했다. 그리고 나는 자주 어지러움을 느끼고 목에 뻐근함이 있다. 의사는 그 증상들이 업무관련 스트레스의 증상이라고 말해주었다. 의사가 스트레스는 정신적으로 신체적으로 해롭다고 말했을 때, 나는 민수 씨가 생각났다. 왜냐하면 그는 전에 업무 스트레스로 병원에 입원한 적이 있었기 때문이다. 나는 건강을 유지하고, 일과 삶의 균형을 유지하기 위해 노력해야겠다고 생각했다.

나이 걱정, 괜한 걱정

앞에서 배운 표현을 활용한 주제별 스피치에 도전!
음원을 들으며 영어문장을 따라 말해보세요.

음원 듣기

I graduated from my university 3 years later than others. I had to retake the university entrance exam because I didn't do well on the test. Also, I took a year off and studied English abroad. After I got back, I spent time working part time. I was worried a lot at first because I thought age is important when getting a job. But from my experience, attitude is more important.

저는 남들보다 3년 늦게 졸업했어요. 시험을 잘 보지 못해서 수능을 다시 봐야 했거든요. 또, 1년을 휴학하고 어학연수를 했어요. 돌아온 후에는, 아르바이트를 하면서 시간을 보냈어요. 처음에는 걱정을 많이 했어요. 직장을 얻을 때 나이가 중요하다고 생각했거든요. 하지만 제 경험으로 볼 때, 태도가 더 중요해요.

새로운 사랑의 시작?!

앞에서 배운 표현을 활용한 주제별 스피치에 도전!
음원을 들으며 영어문장을 따라 말해보세요.

음원 듣기

On Friday night, my coworker Mike texted me. "Do you want to go for a movie tomorrow? A good movie is in cinemas right now." He said Kang Dong-won played the lead role in the movie and his friend highly recommends watching it. I was so excited because I have liked him for the last few years and he has asked me out! I can't believe this! How can I focus on the movie? Oh my god! I think I should dress up tomorrow. I'm super happy and nervous right now.

금요일 저녁에, 동료인 마이크가 나에게 문자를 보냈다. "내일 저랑 영화 한 편 볼래요? 괜찮은 영화가 상영중이래요." 그는 강동원이 영화의 주연이고 그의 친구가 그 영화를 강추했다고 말했다. 나는 너무 들떴다. 왜냐하면 지난 몇 년 동안 그를 좋아했기 때문이다. 그런데 그가 나한테 데이트 신청을 한 것이다. 믿을 수가 없어! 어떻게 내가 영화에 집중할 수 있겠어? 맙소사! 내일은 옷을 잘 차려입어야겠다. 나는 지금 너무 행복하고 떨린다.

미혼 스트레스

앞에서 배운 표현을 활용한 주제별 스피치에 도전!
음원을 들으며 영어문장을 따라 말해보세요.

음원 듣기

Whenever I meet my relatives, I get stressed out because they always ask me, when I will get married. I am just in my early-30s. I think I am still young. Some people are not happy even after they get married. Other people are happy being single. I am not making excuses not to get married. I think there isn't a deadline to getting married.

저는 친척들을 만날 때마다, 스트레스를 받아요. 왜냐하면 그들은 항상 내게 언제 결혼하냐고 묻기 때문이지요. 저는 이제 갓 30대 초반이에요. 제 생각에 저는 아직 충분히 젊어요. 몇몇 사람들은 결혼한 후에 행복하지 않아요. 또 다른 사람들은 혼자라서 행복해하죠. 결혼할 시기를 놓친다는 그런 건 없다고 생각해요.

오랜만에 신혼 느낌

앞에서 배운 표현을 활용한 주제별 스피치에 도전!
음원을 들으며 영어문장을 따라 말해보세요.

음원 듣기

My wife and I went on a date for the first time in 6 months. My mother-in-law took care of our babies for us. We went to a chicken restaurant. We used to go there often before we got married. Chicken was so crispy and draft beer was tasty. My wife said just taking a sip of beer removed all of her stress from raising the babies. She couldn't sleep well because the babies cried a lot in the middle of the night. I felt so sorry because I couldn't do much to help her.

아내와 나는 거의 6개월 만에 데이트를 했다. 장모님이 우리를 위해 아이들을 봐주셨다. 우리는 치킨 집에 갔다. 결혼하기 전에 거기 자주 갔었다. 치킨은 아주 바삭바삭했고, 생맥주는 신선했다. 아내는 맥주 한 모금이 아기들을 키우는 스트레스를 날려주는 것 같다고 말했다. 한밤중에 아기들이 많이 울었기 때문에 아내는 잠을 잘 잘 수가 없었다. 나는 그녀를 많이 도와줄 수 없어서 너무 미안했다.